OWLS

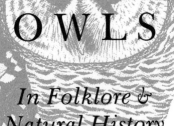

OWLS

In Folklore &
Natural History

Virginia C. Holmgren

Capra Press
SANTA BARBARA

1988

Cover: Little Owl, A. Wilson
Title Page: Barred Owl, A. Wilson
Chapter Heads: Johnstonius

Cover design by Maureen Lauran
Designed and typeset in Baskerville by
Jim Cook/Book Design & Typography
SANTA BARBARA, CALIFORNIA

LIBRARY OF CONGRESS CATALOGING IN PUBLICATION DATA
Holmgren, Virginia C.
OWLS in folklore and natural history / by Virginia C. Holmgren.
ISBN 0-88496-289-x (pbk.) : $8.95
1. Owls. 2 Owls—Folklore. 3. Owls—North America. 4. Birds—Folklore. 5.
Birds—North America. I. Title.
QL696.s8H57 1988   88-15438
598'.97—dc19   CIP

Published by
CAPRA PRESS
Post Office Box 2068
Santa Barbara, California 93120

Table of Contents

Acknowledgements

Very special thanks are due Dr. Peter Davis and family and to photographer Wes Guderian for sharing story and pictures of the Snowy Owl which recuperated in the Davis home; and to John Krussow, Malcolm and Louise Loring, Fern and Frank Sauke and Harvey Steele of the Oregon Archaeological Society for information and photographs of prehistoric rock art; to Eugenio Gavioli of Milan, Italy, and Kim Sasaki of Honolulu for owl lore of their areas; to Danny Bystrak of the U.S. Fish and Wildlife Service for data on owl banding; to Carolyn Cole, John C. Cunningham, James Davis, Jean Foster, Jean Taylor and Karen Kaseberg for information and assistance; to Francis D. Campbell, librarian of the American Numismatic Society and to the libraries of the University of Virginia and University of California at San Diego for lending rare volumes. As alway in my research much is also owed the staff of the Multnomah County Library, Portland, Oregon, for assistance, especially to Clyde Marshall and Douglas Tallman and to the ever-ready Reference Desk crew.

1
OUT OF THE DARKNESS

The cry came out of the midnight darkness, shattering the silence. Two notes. Ominous. Moaning. As menacing as unwarned thunder. Inside the cave the man was instantly awake and on his feet, moving stealthily to the cave opening, testing whether the two-note moans were true owl cry or enemy signal for attack. He listened, waiting for scent or sound of human bodies. Or of something not human? A snarled syllable of rejection rose in his throat. Such fears were for old women and children, not men. Shrugging, he went back to bed.

Beside him the woman reached out to the dried-fern pallet behind her, making sure that First-Born, their son, and Little Sister still slept. Yes, both children were breathing in the steady rhythm of untroubled slumber. But now from the ledge beyond them she heard the old grandmother answering the bird's call with fearful, half-breath query.

"Night-Bird, Death-Bringer, have you come for me?"

As if in reply the voice came again, closer now, and both mother and grandmother gasped. The father roused briefly, muttered and went back to sleep. But First-Born was bolt upright in alarm.

"Who is that?" he demanded in awed wonder.

Before mother or grandmother could speak, the owl seemed to answer for itself, repeating the same two-note moaning cry.

"Oo-hoo! Oo-hoo!"

A shiver spilled down the mother's spine, but she managed to keep her voice calm. "You asked, my First-Born, and she told you. She is Oo-hoo, the Night-Bird. Next time you will know her voice. Now go back to sleep.

"But I have to see her!" the boy protested, ready to head for the cave opening. "And what did Grandmother mean—Death Bringer?"

With a whispery chuckle his mother pushed him back beneath the deerskin coverlet. "Oo-hoo has eyes that see in the dark but you do not, my son. Grandmother can tell you her owl death tales tomorrow. For now—sleep."

PEOPLE OF ANCIENT TIMES all around the world have told stories which linked owls and death. These tales were usually well spiced with magic and mystery, because night-blind humans were amazed at the way owls capture their prey so silently and surely amid utter darkness. Storytellers conjectured that only with magic and witch-craft could the owls hunt so effectively.

The story spread that owls—especially those howling around human dwellings—had once been humans them-selves, turned into night creatures in punishment for their wicked ways. All who doubted this claim were told to look an owl right in the face, to see for themselves that owl eyes are like a human's—both together above rounded cheeks, not one eye on each side of a flat head as in other birds. Witches—also night creatures—were thought to consort with owls as boon companions in evil, both knowing beforetime whenever death and disaster threatened hapless humans. Mournful owl cries might be in sympathy or revengeful gloating but they were seen as true prophecy either way.

So people said and so they believed. And since death and disaster always lurk for the unwary, owl cries in the night were followed by misfortune often enough to give storytellers full chance to nod wisely with an I-told-you-so air. Anyone who saw or heard an owl expected to see a witch, too, if only they dared linger.

Oddly, a male demon was rarely named as owl compan-ion. There seems little reason for this females-only view, since owls of both sexes have almost identical plumage. The female cannot easily be told from the male, even in daylight. The female is usually larger than her mate, but the size difference is not easy to judge unless they are side by side. Nevertheless, owls in many an old legend are presented as female. Several of the world's oldest words for owls also stood for "witch" and were feminine in gender. Among them are *hag* in Anglo-Saxon and Teutonic dialects, *lilith* in Old Testament Hebrew and *strix* in Greek, which became *striga* in Latin. All in all, the witch's role in the mysterious death warnings carried by owl voices has been so deeply embedded in human heritage that its impact is still felt today.

Chances are still good that any one of us, at some dark midnight hour, may be suddenly wakened by a quavery owl cry and feel an inexplicable shiver no conscious thought could have summoned. If the shiver is followed by a strange longing to see the crier and know more of its mysterious ways, then you have a right to suspect that some trace of owl witchcraft lingers among us.

2
THE NAMING OF OWLS

THE OWL WITH THE two-note call was given a name echoing its voice by others besides the cave family. People all around the world have given this kind of owl similar names. And since it ranges over most of Europe and the Middle East, much of North Africa and on across Asia even to Pacific shores, these names are in many languages.

Among the oldest names echoing the owl's cry are *bubo* given by long-dead Romans, *buas* of ancient Greeks, *o-ah* of the Hebrews and *oo-loo* and *goo-goo* in the languages of old India. But you hear the echo in modern names, too, for today's birders like a play-by-ear clue even if this two-noter is more easily identified from guidebook pictures showing its great size, dark brown plumage, big golden eyes and the two feather tufts atop its head like pointed goat horns. In today's German the name is *uhu*, in Dutch *oehoe*, in Italian *gufo*, in Spanish *buho*, and in French *hibou*.

In French, the full name of this particular owl is *hibou*

13

grand-duc. This title of nobility was added during the time when French monarchs were in their glory years, well able to enforce the royal edict forbidding anyone of less than ducal rank to wear erect feather plumes atop hat or headdress lest such adornment make the wearer taller than the king himself. When someone slyly hinted that the big brown night-bird flaunted two such plumes in double disobedience, some more tactful courtier suggested that this owl was obviously of the highest nobility among its own kind or else nature would never have permitted such plumes to grow.

Hibou Grand-duc,
Hibou Moyen-duc and
Hibou Petit-duc, Pierre Belon.

Whether anyone at court really accepted so arrogant—and foolish—an explanation is not on record. Considering the keen French sense of humor, those in the know probably took it as a prime joke common folk never shared. At any rate, the ducal title was officially bestowed and remains in all French bird books. Furthermore, two other tufted owls of middle and small size by owl standards are enrolled as *hibou moyen-duc* and *hibou petit-duc.* All three will doubtless retain noble rank as long as French bird books are published.

If you look for owl names in British bird books you will find no trace of ducal titles. Nor does the English name for this two-note owl hold any resemblance to its call. This particular species has never been more than a rare visitor in the British Isles. The night cries heard in England came from four other species, three of which kept mostly to woods and marsh. But the fourth boldly invaded gardens, barnyards, churchyards and even doorways, announcing itself with a wild and far-carrying cry that could shake any unwarned listeners right down to their boot soles. No two-note moaner, this one. It comes with a screech, a scream, a yell, a yowl, a long-drawn-out shivery shriek. The Englishmen who first tried to put that sound in writing spelled it as *howyelle, uwile, oule, owell, hoole* and similar versions before usually settling on *owl* or *howl* for the bird. *Owlet* and *howlet* were used for the young, and then both *howl* and *yowl* came to mean similar cries by bird, beast or human.

Names with much the same eerie howl label this screamer in other languages. Sanskrit *uluka* and Latin *ulula* are two of the oldest, and among modern names are German *eule*, Dutch *uil*, Spanish *lechuza* and *ugla* or *uggla* in Scandinavian tongues. In time, these names were used for other species, too. But in some countries owlers felt the need of a third name for those owls whose call is half-sneeze, half-bark. Among them are *kauz* in German, *kos* in Hebrew and *chou* or *chouette* in French.

In spite of all these examples, in British and American usage one name now applies to all. An owl is an owl is an owl, whatever the voice, and only some descriptive modifier separates one species from another. The English name for the two-note hooter is Eagle Owl—not intended to suggest actual kinship with eagles but reflecting a similar superiority in size and hunting skill. The eerie-voiced howler now wears the prosaic label of Barn-Owl on official lists. Unofficially it has acquired a picturesque assortment of titles including Bird of Evil Omen, Death Owl, Ghost Owl, Mystery Owl, Knows-all Owl. For many a plain-spoken farmer it is Rat Owl, and with good reason. Some claim you'd need at least a dozen cats to get rid of as many rats as a single Barn-Owl does quite easily.

Not at all oddly, most poets and novelists have preferred

Great Eagle Owle, Francis Willughby.

to identify this rat-catching bird of the smelly barnyard by its soft pastel coloring. That gives two choices, for as the bird flies toward you it looks ghostly white of face, breast and wing linings. Flying away it is a sandy yellow. So white, yellow, silver and gold all can identify just one species for unofficial use, and you have to agree that George Meredith was right to heed his poet's ear when he wrote:

> *Lovely are the wings of the white owl sweeping,*
> *Wavy in the dark lit by one large star....*

However, you can't help thinking that any bird with so fantastic a voice ought to have a name to echo its eerie cry. A good many people, William Shakespeare among them, have agreed and made Screech-Owl their choice. Unfortunately, early English settlers in North America handed over that name to a different owl species, a much smaller bird with both red and gray color phases and wearing ear tufts. This particular bird is found only in the Americas and now, by official international agreement, the label stays in the Americas while the English howler is called Barn-Owl, a name it has worn in English bird books since 1674. Nevertheless, for many a British writer Screech-Owl may still refer to the rat-catcher, a duplication bound to cause confusion.

Luckily official lists set us straight by pairing each local bird name with a two-word scientific label in Latin.

Each species gets its two-word scientific label when a qualified naturalist first publishes a scientific description of the bird. If by chance more than one naturalist publishes such a label, only the first one in public print is official. All the others must be discarded because, since the beginning of the 20th century, naturalists of all countries have agreed to follow that rule. Only this one scientific label is official, no matter how many local names in world languages are in common use.

To determine the most appropriate scientific name, each species is grouped with the other birds it most closely resembles in behavior, appearance and anatomy. These categories in order of closeness are: Class, Order, Family, Genus. Each has its scientific name, and the name for a particular species is made up of the name of the genus plus the name that distinguishes the species itself.

For instance, the scientific description of the Common Barn-Owl is as follows:

CLASS AVES (*aves* is Latin for "birds") a group for all animals with feathers.

ORDER STRIGIFORMES (Latin for "owl-shaped"): a group for all owls and only owls. The distinguishing feature is a wide face with two eyes together above rounded cheeks. Other features unique to owls include eyes fixed in the socket, unable to move sideways, extremely flexible neck muscles and a swivel outer toe able to shift quickly forward or back.

FAMILY TYTONIDAE (perhaps from its mating call "tee-tuh," but probably from Greek *titanos*, "white limestone," plus the family ending *-idae*, Latin for "like"): a group for all owls with <u>pointed</u> chin lines which give them a heart-shaped face. Owls with <u>rounded</u> chin lines are in Family Strigidae. Although all species in this family are not white, they are paler-toned than most other owls.

GENUS TYTO (from Greek *titanos*, "white limestone"): a group for pointed-chinned owls most like the Barn-Owl, the first of the genus to be recorded.

SPECIES ALBA (from Latin for "white"):

SCIENTIFIC LABEL: *Tyto alba,* Common Barn-Owl *(For the scientific labels for all North American owls see Chapter 11)*

How do birdwatchers use scientific terms? Of course all field guides and contemporary texts index the birds by their official Latin names. When researching older books, if you find Screech-Owl in a British reference, the scientific label *Tyto alba* beside it will tell at a glance that this is the Barn-Owl. Knowing the scientific labels will also help if you're traveling abroad using a bird book in a language you don't read.

Tyto Alba, Sir William Jardine.

In Italy, for instance, look up *Tyto alba* in the index and discover a bird named *Barbagianni*, which has nothing to do with barns or owls. A quick check with the dictionary--or the nearest Italian who speaks English— tells you the literal meaning is Johnny Whiskers or Bearded Johnny. Most Italians, however, call it *zio*, meaning "uncle." The nickname may have begun as *zito* or *chio* an echo of typical owl hiss, but *zio* is often a title of respect among countryfolk for white-bearded oldsters, and so the beard instead of the hiss may be responsible and a sort of joke either way.

So score one for the Italian sense of humor. While you're chuckling, you may remember that we often call goats Billy Whiskers. And, goats and owls have something more in common than most people suspect.

In olden times when goats—not more expensive cows—supplied milk for most European families, the herd was brought in from the meadows at dusk for the evening milking. About that time, owls—perhaps Barn-Owls, perhaps some other species—would be emerging from daytime hideaways to begin their evening mouse hunts. As the owl swooped in, the sound of nimble goat feet along the pathway would startle some trembling meadow mouse into a frantic dash right into an owl's out-stretched talons. Hunting with the goat herd became such an easy way for owls to get a quick supper it became a nightly custom for owls in many countries.

Those hoof-beats stir up insects, too, sending them skyward in swarms. And since swarming insects are exactly the food certain other night-birds prefer, they used to join the herds, too, right along with the owls. These insect-eaters were the birds now called nighthawks or nightjars—because they fly like hawks and "jar" the night with shrill, churring cries. Previously they were often miscalled owls, because they share the flying hours of owls. Churr-owls or jar-owls were other common names, or fern owls because they nest on the ground instead of in rocky crevices and hollow trees like most true owls.

Both true owls and jar-owls were given an accusing misnomer—"goatsuckers"—by almost all European farmers with goats to tend. They thought the birds were after milk—not mice or insects—on those plunging dives amid trampling goat feet. And farmers were not alone in making this mistake. Even Aristotle was misled into giving the Barn-Owl such names as *aegotilax* ("goat-sucker") and *aegolius* ("goat-like"). The latter may have been in comparison to the goat's bristly whiskers, but the milk-sucking charge is outright libel for both owls and nightjars.

Nevertheless, nightjars are still listed in Family *Caprimulgidae* (Latin for "Goatsuckers") on official lists and *Aegolius* is the generic label for Saw-whet Owls and Boreal Owls. Today's birdwatchers wonder at the origin of those names but only a century ago almost everyone thought they were accurate—for who could believe that Aristotle was wrong? Besides, the birds could always be observed among the goats.

Goats and owls were remembered fondly by 16th-century Swedish archbishop Olaus Magnus when he moved to Rome to avoid anti-Catholic feeling in Uppsala. There, to ease his homesick longings, he wrote about the animals he had known so well back in northern farm-lands. When his book was finally published in Rome in 1555 it had numerous appealing little woodcuts that have been reprinted many times, including two with goats and owls together.

Olaus Magnus.

One, labeled in his churchman's Latin as "Of nocturnal birds and their food," shows three owls, each with prey in both beak and talons. Chances are neither artist nor author had ever seen an owl fighting two snakes at once or even two rabbits but still wanted to show that owls have two means of attack. Consequently, here they are, fiercely triumphant twice over, and the tufted ears suggest that the Eagle Owl was the species in mind. Sharing the scene are several nightjars, some of them after insects and one stealing that libelous swig of milk from a passive goat.

Olaus Magnus.

The other woodcut, labeled "Of different birds of varying natures," gives center stage to a bristly-headed owl whose facial shape and lack of tufts identify it as the Barn-Owl. A well-bearded goat lurks nearby, suggesting Magnus knew the link between owls and goats even though the name he had learned back in Sweden was *tornuggla,* "Belfry Owl," one more alias for *Tyto alba.*

This confusion of multiple names was about to get a little clarification from a new French book, *L'Histoire de la Nature des Oyseaux,* by Pierre Belon who had earned a medical degree before he turned naturalist. Belon wrote in French instead of the usual scholarly Latin. However, almost anyone with any education then knew some Latin and even a bit of Greek, and so Belon hit on the helpful innovation of identifying each bird with three names: one in Aristotle's Greek, another in Pliny's Latin and the last in contemporary French. Almost any educated European was bound to understand one of those three. The descriptions below the illustrations were in Greek borrowed from Aristotle while the text was in French.

Latinists could check another bird book published that same year, the *Historia Avium* of Conrad Gesner of Zurich whose *Historia Animalium* of four years earlier remained a bestseller. His text was in Latin in keeping with scholarly custom, but like Belon he presented the big owl with the two-note call as the one most likely to be known

Bubo, Conrad Gesner.

to readers by both voice and name. *Bubo* was also the
name most likely to be applied to any other large owl with
tufts anywhere in the world, and it continues to be used as
generic label for all this bird's closest relatives the world
around. It's the clue word if you're wondering whether
any of these cousins are likely to turn up in your own
backyard.

To find the closest relatives for any species, look for
another in the same genus. If no such congeners are listed
in your bird book, then the next best choice is one in the
same family. So begin with checking the index in your
favorite text for any bird in genus *Bubo*.

In American books you won't find *Bubo bubo*. This
Old World wanderer has never crossed either the Pacific or

Atlantic to reach New World shores. But you will find another genus-mate. Throughout all the Americas this next-of-kin is called *Bubo virginianus,* the Great Horned Owl. A glance at the picture shows it to be almost a replica of the European *Bubo bubo.* Both are big and brown-feathered and with those upright "ducal" plumes that give the French *hibou grand-duc* its place among royalty. The American, however, is slightly smaller—just 18 to 25 inches in length instead of the more imposing 25 to 28 inches boasted by *Bubo bubo.*

The *virginianus* was given that specific name because it was first catalogued for science in that state. However, it ranges much farther than the label implies. It is found almost anywhere in the New World from central Alaska on down to Tierra del Fuego, being absent only from the treeless Arctic and Antarctic regions and from a few Caribbean islands farther from mainland shores than most owls care to fly. Its hooting call has much the same deep-throat tone as the "oo-hoo" of its Old World kin, but with four or five syllables, not just two. Ancient Amerind tribes often gave it a name to imitate those moaning syllables, and some of them are still remembered and used today when tribes gather to renew their heritage. Among those echoic names are *hu-tu-tu* from Arawak languages of the Caribbean, *tun-ku-lu-chu* from the Campas of Peru, *te-co-lotl* in Mexico, *pa-cu-ru-tu* from the Tupi people of Brazil. However, the Cherokee people knew the hooter as *tskili*—meaning "witch"—a match for the old European names such as *hag* or *striga,* showing that people can think alike even when half a world apart.

Taxonomists, scientists specializing in giving animals the right scientific label, do not go by the old saying that it's best to let well-enough alone. They're always looking for something better and refining their categories. The latest revision of the *A.O.U. Check-List of North American Birds*—the authority on American bird naming—has at least one change you'll want to mark among owl listings, especially if you're a Westerner.

The Screech-Owl, that little tuft-eared bird almost everybody knows—the one that complicated matters by borrowing the English common name for *Tyto alba* more than two hundred years ago—has now been divided into two species, Eastern and Western Screech-Owls. Plenty of western owlers will assure you full species rank was due their bird long ago.

And might have been given—if John Kirk Townsend of Philadelphia hadn't had two hungry companions on his trek to Oregon back in 1834. Townsend's group found little to eat but rosehips that September day as they crossed Oregon's Blue Mountains. When he shot an owl he thought might be a new species, he hurried back to camp to stash it away for later study and went on with his search for more material for Oregon natural history records. Nothing turned up, so the owl was much on his mind as he came into camp at dusk. And stood there blinking at the little pile of well-picked owl bones beside the campfire and the telltale blend of guilt and contentment on the faces of his two friends. As Audubon put it later—owl meat "is not disagreeable eating," at least not if you're hungry enough.

"So the bird of wisdom lost the immortality which he might otherwise have acquired," Townsend wrote philosophically in his journal. He would be first to enroll several other western birds, have namesakes both in scientific labels and common names, but not this owl.

The total of owl species north of Mexico came to 19 and the world list to 135 in 1983, with the appointment of full species status to the Western Screech-Owl, *Otus kennicotti.* The 134th species had been discovered in 1976 when two ornithologists sponsored by Louisiana State University Museum of Zoology joined Lima museum experts in studying birdlife in a remote cloud-forest of the Andes Mountains in northern Peru. One day they chanced upon a little brown hobgoblin of an owl perched on a mossy branch among trailing orchids and they looked and listened in wide-eyed delight as it tuned up with an eerie, musical whistle.

Xenoglaus loweryii, Bruce Dauner.

Not one of them doubted this six-inch elf was an unlisted species, a true discovery. For one clue, no other owl has such a jutting fringe of whiskery cheek feathers and they could all agree that the name Long-whiskered Owlet gave testimony to both that adornment and small size. For a scientific label, however, three carefully pre-served specimens had to be taken back to Louisiana for a thorough examination by experts, and the verdict was more than satisfying. The hobgoblin was not only an unlisted species but was so different it required a com-pletely new genus.

Xenoglaux loweryii is its label on scientific rolls. The species name honors an admired professor and the generic term combines *xeno*, Greek for "alien", and *glaux*, a Greek name coined especially for another elf-size owl, the very species that long ago in ancient Athens helped make "wise as an owl" a saying that would be repeated the world around for generations to come.

3

BIRD OF WISDOM, BIRD OF DEATH

ANY OWL, WAKENED suddenly from its noonday nap, has to sit blankly staring while its eyes adjust to full daylight, its solemn demeanor managing to make it look as wise as the most learned judge. But that wasn't the way a certain small she-owl in ancient Athens came by its reputation for wisdom.

Athenians already had a friendly feeling for owls of this kind—starling-size, round-headed, with streaked brown plumage and big bright yellowish eyes glaring fiercely at intruders from beneath pale slanted brows. The eyes were what they admired most and they coined a name to match. *Glaux.* To the Greeks it meant a color of the high brilliance seen especially on certain minerals—yellowish-green or greenish-blue-gray—but brightly shining like those eyes, whatever the hue. As the name slipped into general use it carried with it the belief that the very brilliance of those eyes somehow provided an inner light—a magic glow invisible to humans—enabling owls to see clearly in dark of night.

Athene noctua, Sir William Jardine.

Perhaps at first the full name was *glaukopis,* "Shining-Eyed One." But every Athenian knew only the eyes held that namesake radiance. No need to use the complete phrase. *Glaux,* "The Shining One," was name enough.

As yet there was no added name to boast of owl wisdom. But then a she-owl came winging up the Acropolis, the highest hill in all Athens, to the pillared temple recently dedicated to the goddess Athena. A certain half-hidden niche atop one of the tall stone pillars upholding the temple roof became her nesting site. A few windblown leaves were already caught there, as much as she needed for nesting material, and she settled in at once.

She must have had a mate. There must have been eggs to hatch and nestlings to raise. But somehow mate and young were not part of the story as Athenians would tell it in later years. Only the she-owl shared the legend.

Soon she was so much a part of the hilltop scene that Athenians who came to make their prayers and offerings to the goddess expected to see the owl. More than one worshipper made a habit of glancing up at the niche, hoping to see a bobbing head and those two bright eyes shining out of the shadows like gemstones. Even people who did not care for owls let her alone, not wanting to molest any creature in so holy a place.

"She's a wise bird, nesting there," Athenians would say, nodding to each other. "As wise as Athena herself." To them, Athena was the very essence of wisdom. They believed she had been born from the brain of all-wise Zeus himself, father and ruler of the gods; born a maiden full-grown with sword and shield in hand ready to protect her namesake city as Zeus ordained. She was guardian of its homelife, its artisans and—above all—its brave soldiers pledged to defend Athens with their lives.

Soon those who came to the temple were saying Athena had special concern for the welfare of this small owl, that the two were companions, sharing the night hours. In time, most Athenians also believed the owl could serve as the goddess' other self. Artists began portraying the two together, the owl perched on Athena's shoulder or nest-ling in her upturned palm. In the 5th century B.C., silversmiths who designed the city's coins for far-flung trade manufactured a silver tetradrachma showing the goddess on one side and the owl on the other. The owl's eyes were vastly over-exaggerated on the coin to emphasize their importance. What could be more important to an owl than eyes that enable it to see more—and know more—than humans? Too, the shining eyes had given Athena's owl her name.

Athenian coin,
Virginia C. Holmgren.

The coin was soon as valued for its honest weight and worth—a reputation not all monies in Middle East lands could claim—as for its design. But the two female figures—the goddess and the owl—gave the coin its nickname. "The girls," one merchant might say to another, stacking up the coins for counting. And as "the girls" rang true for weight, coin against coin in treasure chest and merchant's till and traveler's moneybag, the story of how the owl came to be pictured with the goddess was told in marketplace, inn and castle in town after town all around Mediterranean shores.

The legend grew that Athena herself would often take the form of her owl companion and go about in feather-clad disguise to learn the needs of her people—and what they knew of rumors a Persian fleet would soon attack Athens. Everyone in Athens had heard some rumor of Persian attack in that troubled year of 490 B.C. The army took what defense measures it could. Posted lookouts along the coast. Stationed added troops in Athens and wherever else danger seemed most likely, sending reserves hither and yon at each new rumor.

Most of Athens' forces were elsewhere that September day when a frantic runner from Marathon came stumbling through the city gates, gasping warning of a Persian fleet coming to anchor near Marathon plains. Forty thousand men, at least, with mounted troops for the dread charge all foot-soldiers feared most.

General Miltiades, left in charge, listened grimly, assessing the odds against him. He could muster a mere ten thousand foot-soldiers, and no horsemen whatsoever. What chance for so few to keep the Persians from riding over them, tromping over them, sweeping on right through Athens gates?

One chance, perhaps. Could he get to the coast soon enough, fight there, give time for Athens to call back every troop possible, even if it meant he'd fight to the last man? As it probably would. . . .

Marching full-pace, they found dusk already closing in as they reached the plain. Too late to start a battle now. Across the grassland the Persians were beginning to set up camp, for the Greeks could see the cookfires even at this distance. Miltiades ordered cookfires, too—but no more soldiers to tend them than must be. All others were to fell trees, gather rocks, stumps, branches—anything to drag down to the plain as snares for the hoofs of the Persian war horses when they charged at full-tilt.

Luckily the moon was just past the full. Bright enough to aid their work but not bright enough to betray them to the Persians, they thought.

Perhaps the Persians saw enough, after all. Something decided them to send the horses off at some distance, to drink and graze. Certainly no general worth his helmet would deprive himself of such advantage—unless it was to save the horses for a surer victory another day, another place.

An Athenian spy came racing back with word—no horses! Attack now, man to man. Even at those four-to-one odds they had a chance now. . . .

Not much of a chance. The Athenians knew it—and kept fighting. Suddenly a shout—another, another. . . .

"Athena! Look up! Athena!"

And there she was above them. A small round-head owl circling in rally call, in promise of victory.

The promise was kept. Soon every Athenian could see the Persians were in full retreat, swarming onto the ships, ready to sail away. The final count would prove they left over six thousand dead on the plain while the Athenians lost only 192.

Battle-wise Miltiades now ordered fast march for Athens, sent his best runner ahead with warning the Persians would be sailing around the cape to attack from the other side. A warning and a plea to hold on, his men were coming, and both arrived so quickly the very name

Marathon would become a watchword for runners through all time to come.

In later years military experts would credit the Marathon victory to the Athenians' longer spears and their breastplates of heavy bronze which protected them better than the Persians' padded cotton. But Athenians gave their tribute to Athena and her owl and the moonlight they brought to guide the workers. If the owl was mentioned more often than the goddess it was only because the two were one—and it was the owl they saw.

So potent was the owl omen that in later years one Greek general—perhaps more than one—kept a trained owl hidden in its cage among his baggage, ready to release whenever its circling presence might make the difference between victory and defeat. Such an owl played a part on stage in the classic drama "The Wasps" by Aristophanes to cheers and applause.

Stories of the victory owl of Marathon were still being told centuries later when the Greeks were finally defeated by invading Roman legions. And even the Romans were impressed. Among their own goddesses was one named Minerva who had much the same role as Athena in sponsoring learning, home crafts and artists. Now they gave her an owl companion, and with it the role of goddess of wisdom. For the Romans and all they conquered the owl was now Minerva's with no debt to Grecian lore acknowledged.

When the Romans went on to rule over most of western Europe, they took the stories of Minerva's wise little owl with them and the stories were told often—and believed. To this day Scandinavians still call the little round-headed owl *Minervauggla,* "Minerva's owl" and consider it a clever bird.

But Romans themselves could not forget their long belief in the owl's role as messenger of death. The first-century naturalist Pliny—whose writings would still be considered the ultimate authority when Christopher

Columbus was preparing for his trans-oceanic voyages—dubbed owls "funereal birds of night" and left his readers in no doubt that they were all birds of ill omen, with tufts or without, large or small.

Roman citizens were said to believe so completely in the prophecy of death brought by each owl cry that they immediately tried to capture the bird and end its life beyond all possibility of revival. Merely wringing its neck was not enough. They also burned the mangled body to a crisp and tossed the ashes into the River Tiber lest even one flake remain. Somehow, they managed to convince themselves that destroying the caller prevented its prophecy from being fulfilled.

Eventually Rome itself was conquered, but the lore and learning it had brought to western Europe remained long after the soldiers and governors had gone. For now Latin became an international language for scholars. All books of importance were in Latin, and since Roman authors had borrowed heavily from the Greeks, European scholars were soon aware that Athena, not Minerva, had first claim on Little Owl companionship and that the bond between them was wisdom.

So now in scholarly writing the name would again be *Athene noctua,* "Athena's night bird," though not without some opposition. Certain British scholars insisted *Carine noctua* would be a better choice, since these owls had been honored by the Carines, people who occupied Grecian shores and nearby islands long before Athens was a city. In proof, experts at the Ashmolean Museum at Oxford showed a tiny carved stone seal in typical Little Owl pose and dated at around 2200 B.C. However, when experts began to argue whether it came from Caria or Crete, the attempt to change the Latin label for the Little Owl was abandoned. There could be no argument about the bond between the owl and Athens—not with all those coins to prove the relationship. But that didn't do away with firm belief in the ability of all owls to predict death and disaster.

Little Owl, Conrad Gesner.

In the British Isles the Little Owl itself had small part in either argument or superstitions. It is not a native species in Britain and was not introduced as a wildling until late in the 19th century when birds brought from the continent were turned loose to survive or perish. They survived—which may have been a testimony to their wisdom as well as to adaptability—but meanwhile few Englishmen got to know this owl really well.

Tawny Owl, Sir William Jardine.   Common Barn-Owl, Conrad Gesner.

The two owls they did know were the Common Barn-Owl—the one with the eerie voice and insatiable appetite for rats—and the Tawny Owl—the woods bird with the brown plumage and the wide-eyed, black-eyed stare. Without anyone ever making conscious choice, the Barn-Owl became the Death Owl and the Tawny the Bird of Wisdom.

Somehow, perhaps because contrariness and resentment of authority are part of human nature, the Tawny also became the symbol of those who bluff their way to a reputation for brain power. When British cartoonists wanted to portray some pompous politician mouthing meaningless nothings, it was usually a black-eyed, round-headed owl that got the role. In the centuries when sportsman's etiquette required each kind of animal to have its own group label, something more fitting than just "herd" or "flock"—as an "exaltation" of larks, for instance, or a "murmuration" of starlings—the owls were said to gather in a "parliament". No one explained—at least not in print—whether those who applied the term thought members of parliament—and therefore owls, also—were actually wise or only tried to look the part with solemn mien and haughty stare. At any rate, slander or compliment, the label was affixed, shared briefly by all owls, and forgotten.

In 1499 when the Bishop Goldwell of Norwich was asked the manner in which owls proved their vaunted wisdom, he described their "safe closeness" and "singular perspicacity" as well as an unexplained "inner light" that guides them at night when humans are blinded. Whether this last phrase came from a sermon or from his translation of the original Greek *glaux* was not mentioned.

Early in the 19th century the poet Alfred Tennyson gave credit to the Barn-Owl (although he called it the White Owl) for using all of a human's five senses with the lines:

> *Alone and warming his five wits*
> *The white owl in the belfry sits.*

In 1791 an earlier anonymous rhymester implied owl wisdom was largely gained by its silence:

> *The grave owl with wisdom fraught*
> *In sober, solemn silence sits.*

34

In 1875 another nameless versifier seconded that opinion with this much-quoted ditty from *Punch:*

> *There was an old owl lived in an oak,*
> *The more he heard, the less he spoke;*
> *The less he spoke, the more he heard;*
> *O, if men were all like that wise bird!*

Meanwhile, Londoner James Northcote had encased the same view in a moral little fable that can be summarized thus:

> *A Barn-Owl was sitting alone and silent as usual in his hayloft hideaway one morning when a talkative jay dropped in for a visit. The jay began sharing his collection of gossip at once, not even pausing for the owl to comment, and kept on with his chatter for an hour or more. When he finally left—still without any remarks from his host—he told all the other barnyard birds he'd never shared a more interesting and enjoyable conversation.*

Since fabulists of those days always explained the moral, lest it be missed by careless readers, Northcote added that the best way to become known as a fine conversationalist was to let your companion do all the talking. He also cautioned that the tongue "is a wild beast very difficult to be chained once let loose." A nugget of wisdom owls have apparently learned well and practice faithfully for good example to humans.

A few years later the renowned ornithologist Alfred Newton, writing for *The Encyclopaedia Britannica,* insisted the Little Owl had no claim to wisdom whatsoever. It was in his opinion a "veritable buffoon" given to "grotesque actions" and "ludicrous expressions." An odd opinion for a man of science and one that ignores the definition for wisdom endorsed by both contemporaries and ancients. Today's reliable Merriam-Webster declares wisdom the ability to make discerning judgments—an idea apparently in circulation since the days of King Solomon.

Anyone who watches owls knows the birds make judgments—even life-or-death judgments—every day. Time and again, and often in one split second they must choose to fly or sit tight when an enemy appears. And if they sit—is the next choice to challenge the intruder or slip away? If that intruder is a snake, is it small enough to kill and eat or too big to tackle safely? Each spring they must choose which partner makes the best mate, which site the safest nest. Every night on hunting foray they must choose their tactics—a swoop to right or left or straight down upon a mouse about to flee in panic.

Some of these judgments—and others—are decided partly by their inherited reflexes without conscious choice. But not all. The owl brain is proportionately as large or larger than that of a rodent. It is well-equipped with association centers which enable the owl to relate result to cause—as they do in learning to follow grazing animals for a bounty of disturbed insects. In many other actions there is also choice, judgment, wisdom. Or so most of us who watch owls believe.

Like every other owl watcher, the author has her own favorite tale of one owl's wise judgment. Come with me into the kitchen to watch in wonder and surprise as I did on one never-forgotten evening in late October, just before Halloween. Stand beside me as I light the gas under the teakettle. Glance out the windows and we can see the dusk beginning to close in and. . . .

What was that sound? Listen! Do you hear it? That odd noise coming from inside the oven?

"Scritch-scratch! Scratch-scritch!"

I opened the oven door and there he sat. A wide-eyed gray Screech-Owl, head tilted with puzzled air as if he were still trying to figure where he made the wrong turn. Instead of scrambling back up into the open air he had just kept on going down the stove pipe into this strange place of darkness—and now glaring light. With a human!

Puzzled, yes. But not frightened. He sat there front and

center, toes curled around the very middle of the shelf's top rung.

I dashed to close the doors to the rest of the house, remembering how other uninvited bird visitors had careened in panic from wall to window to doorway. But no panic for this one. Even when I opened the door wide for unobstructed exit—he continued to sit watching me with that wide-eyed stare as if the next move were definitely up to me.

I thought of trying to pick him up at the shoulders and toss him out the door as I'd learned to do handling a friend's racing pigeons. But a glance at his hooked beak and talons suggested I'd better find another way.

Suddenly I knew. Was it all those orange-and-black Halloween streamers I'd been seeing in the shops? Owls and bats and witches riding on broomsticks. . . .

I grabbed the broom and held it out to him straw-end first. And he stepped aboard! Calmly, sedately, as if he had been riding on broomstraw all his life. Sat quietly, not even ruffling a feather as I carried him, broom at arm's length, across the kitchen, across the porch, until he was at last free and clear under the night sky. Now—judgment told him—he was safe to fly away, and off he flew, a gliding, wide-winged shadow.

Looking back, I know it was not judgment but blurred vision under the glaring light that kept him quiet at first. And I suspect it was the straw tips tickling the back of his toes that nudged him forward onto the broom so promptly. Nevertheless, he could have squawked in protest, skittered about the room, tried to find the way out on his own. But he didn't. So for me he's still a Wise One.

Of course everyone with a wise-owl tale to tell has another of an owl not so wise. Have you heard of the Burrowing Owls of Midland, Texas, who couldn't tell the difference between their own eggs and a golf ball?

Whether male or female was the ignoramus—or both— is not certain. Both share in incubating the eggs and both look alike to humans. Besides, neither deserves condemnation for the mistake since eggs and golf balls are both white, both roundish, both about the same size. And these new round white things kept turning up at the burrow door, and what was an owl to do except nudge them on down the tunnel to where their replicas lay side by side?

Meanwhile, human owners of those vanished balls couldn't have been so all-wise either. For by the time someone thought to search the burrow, the owls had 27 balls piled up tidily beside their junior "parliament" of just-hatched owlets.

Wise or not, Burrowing Owls share this chapter with Athena's bird, for the two are now listed in the same genus. Before 1983 revisions, the Burrower was alone in genus *Speotyto*, a label that falsely implied close kinship with the Barn-Owl. Now, as *Athene cunicularia*, Athene's Little Rabbit-hole User, it is the only Little Owl congener in the Americas. Americans now have a chance to see an acknowledged look-alike for the bobbing head and bright yellow eyes in a round brown-feathered face that once peered down at Athenians from the temple niche on Acropolis hill.

The Burrower has no goddess counterpart to keep it "one of the girls." Most of its nicknames turn out to be masculine: Billy Owl, Little Miner, Tunneler. But Burrowing Owls, like Athena's Little Shining Ones, are generally welcomed as friends by human neighbors. They are seldom burdened with the onus any larger owl still endures as messenger of death, omen of evil, as it has through the ages, the world around.

In supposedly staid and sensible England the fear of owls — especially the Barn-Owls — as Death Bringer endures to the present century. It might be strongest among countryfolk, but the fear was equally prevalent among city sophisticates and scholars only a few centuries ago.

Among those who shivered when owls called from nearby post was the famous poet Geoffrey Chaucer, who wrote in 1385 that they were prophets of "wo and mys-chance"—a comment that gets its meaning across in spite of the individualistic spelling that goes with Chaucer's era. Two centuries later another English poet, Edmund Spenser, would name the owl "death's dread messenger." Shakespeare set the same ominous tone with the phrase "the fatal bellman."

Shakespeare also had an owl or two hooting dire death warnings or adding a gloomy aura in almost every play he wrote. If he happened to omit the owl's warning omen, stage managers used to call out with off-stage howl themselves, or get some reedy-voiced stagehand to attempt an imitation of the Barn-Owl's banshee wail. Either way, the attempts were often less than successful, so obviously faked that certain light-spirited young blades in the audience felt constrained to supply a better rendition. Applause or calls of derision--or both—from the rest of the audience often ruined the scene for serious listeners and so the off-stage sound effects were quickly abandoned. But belief in owl calls as death omen was not so quickly erased.

As late as 1887 the English scholar John Ruskin wrote that whatever others might say of owls' link with disaster, he himself had always found them to be "prophets of mischief." Perhaps he thought the term "mischief" mild enough to absolve him from being condemned as heretic or simpleton or whatever label of scorn might be applied, but the odor still clings.

Meanwhile, among the Hindu villages in the province of Hyderabad in central India, any owl had come to be an omen of death and calamity. If one of them came near a house or outbuildings it was killed at once—if possible. And if it had actually perched on the roof, the thatch was immediately stripped from the rafters and burned. No one even thought of going back into the house until new thatch was in place.

Much the same belief set villagers in parts of China to

shivering whenever an owl was even heard, whether seen or not. For in this area the eerie notes were no subtle hint of misfortune. In the local dialect the *hoo-oo-hoo-oo* syllables were taken as a terrifying and unmistakable death threat since they were a perfect match for the very words: *Go dig your grave!*

Common Barn-Owl, Sir William Jardine.

4
OWLS IN AMERICAN
INDIAN LEGENDS

IN THE AMERICAS of long ago, the people of the tribes listened when the owl called. To them the owl served the Great Spirit and shared in the god's supernatural powers. For many tribes the owl's special role was as a messenger to warn them of coming death. But almost everyone believed the owl had other mysterious power as well.

How could they think otherwise? A bird with almost human face, magic see-in-the-dark eyes, ghostly voice, and an incredible way of soundlessly swooping on its prey was bound to be linked with mystery. And bound to be given added respect if it were also bedecked with upright feather head plumes, the Indians' own status symbol.

The two most abundant and widespread species with feather tufts atop their heads—usually the Great Horned Owl and a Screech-Owl—were the ones most often given

The Horn Owle, Francis Willughby.

a leading role in Indian owl legends. These two—or any
other owl—might appear in dream or vision to anyone.
Usually the most revered of the tribal leaders, the one
entrusted to serve as both doctor and priest, healer of both
body and soul, was the only one to approach the owl and
ask for guidance.

Each tribe had its own language; therefore the word for
such a doctor-priest was different in each linguistic group.
But early European settlers were confused at hearing so
many different names for the same thing—and even more
confused at the idea of having one man be both doctor and
priest. So instead of adopting any Indian word, they just
used one of their own. For the French it was *médecin,*
"doctor." The English chose *medicine man.* Both ignored
the religious part of this elder's duties, mostly because the
Indian religious rites often seemed more like magic than
any European church service.

However, English explorers in Asia a century later
found Oriental tribes with doctor-priests, too, known as
shamans. For some reason, this word seemed acceptable
while American words with the same meaning had not,
and it was commonly used in English travel books as early
as 1698. Eventually, English travelers in the Americas

began using it in their writings instead of medicine man and it is still the choice of many writers today. Although *shaman* was never used by American tribes, it carries the correct dual meaning and so it will be used in the owl legends retold here.

Come, then, to a council fire of a Pima tribe in what is now Arizona on a long-ago evening when the talk had been of the tone of real anguish, deep heart-felt suffering, that could be heard in the owl's call that came as death warning.

The fire was burning low now and the talk, too, had lost its spark when a Pima elder gave words to the thought that so far had been only unspoken undercurrent.

"What you are asking," he said, "is this—Is it possible the owl's sad tone is trying to let us know it shares our sorrow at the death it must foretell?"

There were nods all around the circle, and then, almost as one, they turned to look at the shaman.

The shaman thought for a moment and then spoke.

"It is possible."

Plainly he was waiting for the elder to continue speaking for the others, to complete the question they were all asking in their hearts.

"Then," the elder began slowly, "perhaps the owl is willing to ease our death journey. For us, the way from Here to the Hereafter is dark and dangerous. For us it is unknown, unknowable. But surely the owl, who already can travel safely through the darkness of night, knows the way through the darkness of death, also. Do we dare ask him to go with us on death journey? To guide each Pima safely when the time comes? Is that possible?"

"It is possible," the shaman said at last, "if we ask with fitting reverence. At the right time and place and with the right words."

And since he was the only one able to choose time and place and words, he went off to wait for the dream that would show him how the petition should be made. When he was sure he understood the dream's message he called two of his helpers to him to explain what they must do. One would go east, the other west, each alone and with prayerful heart, seeking an owl willing to listen when a Pima spoke. They were not to ask the all-important question—that would come later— merely greet the bird with reverence and wait to see if it stayed to listen or flew away. If it did not take wing, then it would listen when the request came with proper ceremony.

The two apprentice shamans went off eagerly, one east, one west, just as the dream had directed. And as it happened, both returned at almost the same moment.

"I found the Great Owl, T'-co-kon-du," said the one who had gone eastward. "He did not speak to me in answer to my greeting. But he did not turn aside or fly away. And his great yellow eyes met mine without anger. Is not that proof we may ask him?"

The shaman did not answer but only turned to the one who had gone westward and was obviously eager to tell his story.

"I found Ko-ko-vol, the Little Gray Owl," he said proudly. "When I greeted him he made little clicking sounds, as if he were shaking a gourd rattle as we do in our prayer dances. Is not that proof we may ask him?"

Again everyone had to wait for the shaman to think before he spoke.

"We will ask them both," he decided.

Everyone knew they would have to wait until he had dream guidance of the next step, and they could hardly manage to keep from giving their own opinions on the how and where of matters while they waited. At last they were invited to come together in council circle and listen.

Some among them had been given special ceremonial baskets beautifully woven of maguey leaves, and they held them like drums, softly stroking them with hand-slap beat. Now one of the shaman helpers, the one known as a

*Singer of Songs, stepped forth quietly and began swaying
to the tempo set by the whisper-music of the baskets, as
soft as one owl feather swishing against another. Softly,
softly, he began his prayer song:*

> *Hear us, Small Gray Owl!*
> *Hear us, Great Owl!*
> *Two alike with upright plumes.*
> *Two alike who know death's darkness.*
> *Hear us, Ko-ko-vol!*
> *Hear us, T'-co-kon-du!*

*Then he lifted both arms high, to the east, to the west.
And all the Pimas knew they must now send up their own
prayer, silently, with words heard only in their own
hearts. When the whisper-music stopped, they knew their
prayer had been heard and an answer would come. All
they could do now was wait.*

*It was the Small Gray Owl who answered first. Sud-
denly one evening he was there at the edge of the village,
and he came again for three evenings in a row. The next
night the Great Owl came. Though the Pimas were sure
now that both owls would serve as guide on death
journey, they believed the Gray Owl would come more
willingly and they listened eagerly to him shaking his
gourd rattle as goodwill sign.*

*"Listen when the owl calls," parents would tell their
children. "Listen with respect, for he may one day be your
guide."*

*And one oldster would say to another, "The owl will
call for me any day now. He will guide me safely. I will
have no fear."*

Pimas would not say so aloud, but some of them dared
hope they themselves would become owls as they took
death journey and be able to return and guide others. This
was part of Pima belief now. It was also Pima custom to
place an owl feather in the hand of one about to die so the

owl might see it and know this one was ready for the journey.

Not just any owl feather would do. It had to be one dropped by a living owl at one's door or along a much-used path, as if on purpose. Each family was supposed to make a collection of such feathers to have ready when needed. Of course the shaman had others to use, kept in a special basket of maguey leaves or in a box decorated with the maguey-leaf design.

To ensure himself a steady supply of owl feathers, the shaman usually kept a live owl as a pet, taking a bird from the nest while it was still very young. If a live owl was not available, a stuffed one, carefully perched on a branch in lifelike pose, would do. Sometimes a stuffed owl was the favored choice, especially if the shaman could throw his voice and thereby guarantee that the desired omen would come when called for.

In time, all kinds of tales were told of owls who came at just the right moment to save some Pima warrior from defeat. One snatched the bow right out of the enemy warrior's hand. Another raked an enemy's arm with sharp claws, stripping off enough flesh to make a belt.

If by some evil chance a Pima angered an owl with lack of respect, the transgressor would surely be seized with fits. A cure would come only if you begged the owl's pardon with a ceremonial salute given with a specially prepared prayer-stick adorned with six owl feathers. And woe betide you if the feathers were not from the kind of owl you had offended.

Sometimes the owl death cry came only moments before death itself. But sometimes it came early enough so one had time to prepare, or even to cry out in protest that it was too soon. Pima songs set down in later years gave the very words that had come in protest and fear, and then acceptance, to one Pima on an evening long ago:

Gray Owl came to me at sunset,
Came just as the last rays faded,
Sang to me of death's dark journey,
Sang on, as I froze in terror,
As I cried out for the sunlight
While I saw the last rays vanish,
While Small Gray Owl stood beside me
Clicking, clicking his gourd rattle.

The Pimas may have been the only Amerind tribe to use the owl feather as part of the traditional deathbed ritual. However, many tribes counted the owl as proper companion for the shaman, his link with the supernatural world and a messenger of death. From America's colonial years on through the early 19th century when some tribes could still be found observing their old ways, many a traveler wrote in his journal of the owl's part in ceremonial rites.

In 1791 when naturalist William Bartram of Philadelphia set out to study flora and fauna from the Carolinas to Florida, he happened to visit a Creek village while apprentice shamans were putting on a display, perhaps demonstrating that they were now ready to take on doctor-priest duties. Each one had his owl companion—a Great Owl, Bartram noted, and his description lets us join him as he watched their parade:

Among the Creeks, the junior priests or students constantly wear a white mantle, and have a Great Owl skin cased and stuffed very ingeniously, so well executed as almost to appear like the living bird, having large, sparkling glass beads, or buttons, fixed in the head for eyes. This insignia of wisdom and divination they wear sometimes as a crest on top of the head; at other times the image sits on the arm, or is borne on the hand. These bachelors are also distinguished from other people by their taciturnity, grave and solemn countenance, dignified step, and singing to themselves songs or hymns in a low, sweet voice as they stroll about the town.

In 1832 the German prince, Maximilian of Wied, traveled from Niagara Falls to Mandan Country on the Upper Missouri River and reported that shamans in both Mandan and Minitari (Hadatsa) tribes kept owls—alive or stuffed—as companions and interpreters of supernatural messages. So did Menomini shamans in what is now Wisconsin. Similar reports came from others who visited the Kiowas of the Great Plains.

One Kiowa shaman was well known for the messages brought him by his owl companion even after its death. The owl skin had been prepared with the usual supreme skill the Europeans envied. In addition it was adorned with a bright red sash as a badge of honor and further decorated with numerous trinkets, perhaps gifts from grateful Kiowas who had profited by its warnings. There it sat in splendor from dusk to dawn perched on a pole in front of the shaman's tepee. When the villagers were asleep, the shaman kept watch beside the owl. He told of live owls bringing messages in the silent language that only the owls—and the shaman—understood. Thus forewarned he could give his people the expert advice they expected from him. Along North America's eastern seaboard, Cherokee shamans counted on three owl species for information. The Great Horned Owl, Barred Owl and Eastern Screech-Owl were all valued as consultants. But the Great Owl must have been considered in closest contact with the spirits, for it was known as *tskili*, the "witch," the "magic maker," while the others were usually named only by imitation of their usual call. *U-gu-ku* named the Barred Owl, while the smaller Screech-Owl was *wa-hu-hu*. However, all three seemed equally feared for their power to bring sickness down upon any Cherokee deserving punishment. An owl need only hover overhead so that its wide-wing shadow fell upon the trembling figure below and the curse would be fulfilled.

Even tribes that did not regularly ask their shamans to consult with owl interpreters would often decorate prayer sticks, ceremonial headdresses and other regalia with owl feathers. Feathers—the one thing all birds have that other creatures do not—were always respected for their role in the miracle of flight. Owl feathers added all the potency that belongs to owls alone, especially the foreknowledge of death.

In Argentina, naturalist William Hudson was surprised to find that Indian tribes of the pampas hated and feared the little Burrowing Owls making their underground homes beside the grasslands. To the Indians these small birds with the long legs and bulging eyes were evil personified—and all female. "Sisters of Evil" was their Indian label. The tribesmen killed every "sister" they could see as if it were the worst enemy, and they refused to camp for the night wherever any Burrower had made its home.

About the same time Hudson was making this observation in his Argentine journal, the British naturalist Sir John Richardson was noting that a party of Scottish Highlanders serving with the Hudson's Bay Company in Canada were equally averse to sharing night campsite with an owl. This happened to be a Great Horned Owl, and the men had just begun banking their campfire for the night when its low and dismal notes came from a nearby grove. No one among them had ever heard this American species before, so it was easy enough to imagine it some mysterious spirit—especially when one or two of the boldest among them discovered that the grove also sheltered an Indian grave. Somehow they shivered through the night, but the first faint rays of daylight found them well on their way elsewhere.

Sir John also brought back the description of a small roundhead owl sometimes mistaken for the American equivalent of Athena's Night-bird. Although still listed in older British and American books as Richardson's Owl, the official name is now Boreal Owl, but to Cree Indians of those northern lands it was the Death Bird. In spring courting time, the male often gives a series of peculiar whistles that to Cree ears sounded like a summons from whatever spirits held their lives in thrall. Somehow they came to believe that if they answered the summons with a duplicate whistle—and heard no call in return—their own death would come, and soon, beyond all doubt.

The slightly smaller Saw-whet Owl — another round-head—probably shared the same ominous role in Indian belief. These beliefs were so strong they could actually cause the unanswered whistler to die if a powerful shaman did not intercede. However, the shaman, and his own owl companion, could try to change the verdict and thus avert a death.

5

WHAT OWL WATCHERS
WANT TO KNOW

WHEN YOU WATCH OWLS, learn a little of their ways, all
kinds of questions about them come to mind. And the
more you watch, the more questions you have. Here are
the questions that have been asked most often, each with
answers, some from modern science and others from folklore.

□ *Why do owls have so many splotches and*
  speckles on their dull-colored feathers?

TODAY'S ANSWER:
  Today, speckled feathering is explained with a single
word— camouflage. The word came into English from the
French and means the disguising of some object by break-
ing up its easily-recognized outline into strange-shaped
patterns and unaccustomed colors so that it doesn't look

like itself at all, at least not to an enemy or predator watching from a distance for an easy target.

Nature has been practicing camouflage since the beginning of time by giving animals streaked and spotted and speckled coats in all sorts of crazy-quilt designs. Primitive hunters copied animal disguise, but modern armies have used it only since World War I when French artists taught French generals how to disguise their cannons and fortifications and even the soldiers themselves with misleading patterns enemy pilots overhead would not recognize. Though camouflage itself is a very old idea, the word did not appear in English print until 1917 when London newspapers broke the news about the new military strategy. Soon France's enemies—as well as her allies—were using camouflage, too, but it may still fool even those who expect it.

Burrowing Owl, John James Audubon.

Another camouflage trick nature uses is to give animals coloring that blends in with their usual background. For woods owls that means colors to blend with the browns and grays of the tree trunks they lean against for daytime naps. Burrowing Owls and Short-eared Owls need the lighter tones of dry meadow grasses and bare earth surrounding their nests, dappled to match the effect of bright sunlight since these two ground-nesters are often abroad by day. Indeed, the Burrowing Owl spends so much time sitting beside its tunnel doorway that it needs the most camouflage dappling of all, and Zuñi Indians of long ago concocted an incredible tale to explain nature's fool-the-eye trickery for the Burrower's protection.

AN ANSWER FROM ZUÑI LORE:

In those long-gone days of old when all the world was new, Burrowing Owls got along well with almost all their neighbors. They could dig their own underground tunnel if necessary, but they thriftily preferred use of any aban-doned burrow made by prairie dog, armadillo, gopher or any other sturdy digger who had prepared a home to suit Burrower needs. If a rattlesnake chose to occupy another abandoned tunnel next door, the owls got along with the snake, too, since they all minded their own business and never harmed neighbors who did likewise.

But the Coyote was not so good at minding his own affairs. He always wanted to know what everyone else was doing and why—and he was usually ready to boast that he could do it better. One day he happened to come along just as Grandfather Burrowing Owl was teaching the latest batch of grandchildren how to do the odd little hop-step dance that is a Burrowing Owl specialty.

"Ho-ho-ho," laughed the Coyote. "Aren't you the clumsy ones! I could do your dance better than you any day."

Now it is true that Burrowing Owl babies look clumsy. Their spindly bare legs stick out at awkward angles no matter how hard they try to look graceful. You would almost think their legs had been broken and mended themselves with a crook in each joint. But they try so hard you have to admire them, and in those days they had handsome all-black plumage, too. So there they were all in a row beside the tunnel doorway, bobbing and bowing as Grandfather Owl directed and holding their heads so straight not one spilled even a drop of the yucca plant foam brew in the bowl balanced on each head.

"Give me a bowl," Coyote demanded.

53

Grandfather Owl thought for barely a half-moment. "All right. But first you must break your hind legs so they will be crooked like ours or you cannot match our steps."

"Why not?" Coyote agreed without really listening. By then it was too late to back down. Besides, he couldn't stand being outdone by anyone. So he picked up a stone and gave each leg bone a good crack. Somehow he managed to hobble over and join the line of owl grandchildren, holding on to his bowl with firm paw.

But dancing was something else again. He lopped, he flopped, he staggered and stumbled, reeled this way and that, bumping into one owl child after the other, spattering them with the foam from his bowl in splotches and splashes. And the children were soon laughing so hard at his stumbling antics that their own bowls tilted and slid, splashing them still more with the grayish-whitish yucca foam and leaving a great wide blob of it under each chin like a foam bib.

Nothing could take away those foam splotches and so all Burrowing Owls have worn their speckled plumage ever since. As it turned out, Coyote's legs mended nicely and so he and all coyote-kind after him have been as quick-footed and nimble as ever, and will remain so as long as they go on four legs and leave two-legged dancing to those who have only two legs in the first place.

☐ *Why do owls fly at night?*

AN ANSWER FROM THE MENOMINI TRIBE:

As all Menomini storytellers used to explain, the idea of total night darkness has to be blamed on To-to-ba the Saw-whet Owl. Before the owl interfered, the world knew neither night nor day as we do, but lived in continual grayish half-light. And both To-to-ba and Wa-bus the rabbit complained about this half-light constantly—but for opposite reasons.

"Too dark! Too dark!" Wa-bus would say, wiggling his

nose in disgust with every word. "Too dark! Too dark! Too dark! I wish the world would be bright and light all the time. It would be better for everybody."

And from a branch over the rabbit's head To-to-ba would hiss contradiction. "Not ssssso! Not ssssso! Darkness is best! I wish for darkness, everywhere and forever. Dark, dark, dark!"

Almost at the same moment these two had the same idea, and off they went as fast as they could to ask the Great Spirit for this favor. And almost at the same moment each stopped and looked at the other, for they realized that even the Great Spirit could not give both of them what they wanted. It was not fair to ask the Spirit to decide between them. Instead, they would have a contest. Wabus would ask all the animals who preferred light to come and stand beside him, while all those in favor of darkness would stand beside Totoba. Then, each with his supporters to see all was done fairly, the contest would begin. Wabus would shout out Wabon! Wabon! (Light! Light!) as loud and fast as he could, and Totoba would shout for darkness—Uni-tipt-qkot! Whoever was first to miss and say the other's word instead of his own would lose the contest and win the right to go to the Great Spirit.

"Wabon" Wabon!" shouted the rabbit.

But the word for night was so long that the owl barely managed to say it once before the rabbit had shouted for light three times. And before the owl could take a breath and try again his tongue was so twisted it just stopped of itself and began shouting for light.

"We win!" shouted all those who stood with the rabbit. And the owl had to admit that was so. But the rabbit's nose was twitching faster than ever before as he tried to stop the shouting. "NO! NO! The contest was not fair. Your word was too difficult to say. So we'll both win. We will have light part of the time and dark the rest of the time. Then we'll all have what we want at least part of the time. Agree?"

55

"Agree! Agree!" all the animals shouted together. The Great Spirit agreed also and so the world had night and day, dark and light. And although almost no one remembers to give the rabbit any credit, all those who dislike the dark always blame the owl, not just the little Saw-whet but all owls of every kind and size, for they are all creatures of the night and understand night darkness better than anyone else.

AN ANSWER FROM GERMAN FOLKLORE:

How old is this Old World tale? When was it first told? No one knows. But it was first written down around 1812 when two German brothers—Jacob and Wilhelm Grimm —were trying to collect all the old folk and fairy tales they had heard and loved as children and print them in a book so they wouldn't be forgotten. Until the Grimms got to work, very few of the old tales had been published, but they had been told and re-told by many different people and not always in the same words, and they have been told and re-told, written and re-written ever since.

As it happens, an owl was not the central figure in this story. As it begins, owls had no part at all except that a certain she-owl was one of many birds who had been called together for a meeting because some among them thought one bird ought to be chosen to rule as king. When it was decided that the king would be the bird who could fly the highest, the owl went off to her favorite napping tree, for she was not a high flier and knew she'd never win.

Most of the other birds wanted to be in on the race, win or lose, and so up into the sky they all went—crows and larks and sparrows and the eagle and even a little no-color bird no one seemed to know by name. What a flittering and fluttering they all made! Up, up, up. Higher, higher, higher. Then one by one they began to tire and come dropping back to earth until at last only the eagle could be seen as he mounted higher and higher still.

Now the eagle looked around—below him, above him, on either side—but no other bird was in sight. Confident that he had won and need go no higher, he wheeled in midair, ready to plunge back to earth in a magnificent headfirst dive. Just then he felt something on his back twitch and twirl as the little no-color bird sprang up from its hiding place among the eagle's feathers and took three quick wingbeats higher than the eagle had soared.

"I am king!" the little one cried as he plunged back to earth at the eagle's side. "I flew highest! Even the eagle will admit it! Crown me! Crown me!"

When the eagle explained the trickery, all the other birds were as angry as the eagle himself and all agreed the trickster must be punished. Before they could decide the penalty, the would-be king slipped from the circle and vanished down a mouse hole under a stump and was out of sight, out of reach, before a single bird could move to stop him.

"Well, so he's chosen his own prison," the eagle said, and all the others agreed their prisoner would be safe there till morning. They could all go home and get a good night's sleep and leave the she-owl in charge since night-time was her day-time and she could see in the dark besides. So they routed the owl out of her nook and left her to guard the mouse hole.

Now the owl had not had her full sleep, so she thought she'd just close one eye for a sort of half nap. But somehow the other eye closed, too, for a moment—just long enough for the little bird to scoot out and away—and when the birds re-assembled next morning they had no one to punish. Oh, but they were furious! They turned on the owl ready to pull her apart feather by feather, but they were too angry to see straight and they all got in each other's way and in such a muddle that the she-owl was able to slip away to her roosting hole and keep out of reach.

But not a bird living has ever forgotten they owe the owl

a beating. Since they know just one of them could never do the job, they gang up together whenever they see any owl in daylight and keep chasing till it finds a hideyhole. So owls fly only by dark and dusk now, when other birds are asleep, to avoid the mobbing. And owls also kill every mouse they see, for if that mouse hole hadn't been handy, the little bird would have had no place to hide and the owl would never have been set to guard it. But the little bird did find the hole—and escaped besides—and so it was given a golden crown and dubbed kinglet, although none of the other birds has ever obeyed its orders or recognized it as rightful monarch.

AN ANSWER FROM ALEXANDER WILSON:

Plenty of folk-tales about birds were still being told and plenty of superstitions charged to the owl's night-time habits in the years from 1803 onward when Alexander Wilson first began studying and painting American birds. Yet Wilson managed to take a factual view, putting legend and superstition completely aside in his introduction to the ways of the Great Horned Owl with this comment: "Nothing is a more effectual cure for superstition than a knowledge of the general laws and productions of nature.... With all the gloomy habits and ungracious tones of the owl, there is nothing in this bird supernatural or mysterious, or more than that of a simple bird of prey formed for feeding by night like many other animals and reposing by day."

Luckily, today's viewpoint lets us agree with Wilson on the need for facts yet we can still enjoy the oldtime fantasies for their charm and inventive solutions to nature's puzzles.

☐ *What special advantages help owls hunt at night?*

By day or night, owls use the same five senses we all share. Their sharp hooked talons and a reversible outer toe strengthen their sense of touch with a firm grip diurnal predators cannot match. Sense of smell and taste are weak but come most strongly through the mouth and so warn them to reject putrid carrion before they have a chance to gulp it down. But the three factors that count most in nocturnal survival are these:

—eyes of unique design for absorbing and reflecting light

—ears of supreme sensitivity to sound

—feather structure ensuring swift and silent descent upon prey

OWL EYES ARE UNIQUE. The eyes of owls—like our own and those of most mammals— have three main parts: lens, iris and retina. The lens enables the eyes to focus on a chosen area. The iris opens and closes at its center forming a pupil to control the amount of penetrating light. The retina "photographs" the area in focus and transfers the scene to the brain for evaluation. This image will be in color, for the retina contains two types of cells: rods and cones. Rods are sensitive to black and gray while cones react to brighter colors.

Owl eyes differ from ours in having at least seven times as many rods and cones. The rods are especially numerous, giving owls a much clearer picture than we get in dim light. Also, owl eyes relay the image to the brain faster than human eyes do and are especially prompt in detecting movement. The bulging, tubular shape of owl eyes enables the pupil to absorb more light than flatter human eyes can accept, and much of what looks blackest of black to us will be grayish to owls. Also, most owl eyes reflect the light that reaches the retina as if from a mirror, so it can enter again, thus giving twice the illumination human eyes would have in the same situation. Considering this last factor particularly, you might conclude that the old Greek theory of a magic "inner light" giving owls their nocturnal vision isn't far from the truth after all. Those owl watchers of ancient Athens were right in believing added light must come to owl eyes from somewhere. They just didn't know how it worked.

Owl eyes also have an organ called a pecten which birds and reptiles have but humans do not. It helps keep the eyes healthy, moist and active.

The eyes of songbirds, owls, and humans all contain iris, lens, and retina, but they differ in shape and proportionate size (Oregon Dept. of Fish and Wildlife).

Experts conclude that owl night vision can be at least fifty times clearer than humans can manage, at least for black and gray scenes. Owls must also see some color distinctions at night, but they apparently cannot distinguish between red and surrounding blackness. To establish this point a British ornithologist hung a red lantern over the opening to a Tawny Owl nest hole where parents were making many late-night trips feeding young. The parents ignored the lantern as if it were not there, whereas they would not have ignored a light they could see. Along with proving nocturnal red-blindness in owls, this test also revealed these owlets were fed largely on earthworms—an item not previously observed on owl menus. Since then, numerous watchers have reported owls of many species homing with a beakful of the squirmers.

Even by day owls probably don't see colors as clearly as we do, although tests have indicated they can distinguish the primary colors of red, blue and yellow as well as green. They are not blind in daylight as many people around the world have believed, although day-blind owls have been ridiculed long and often in folklore and literature. The Maya Indians of Mexico, for instance, explained that the owl was doomed to blindness in bright sunlight as punishment for his "bad manners" in staging a temper tantrum at a party after being ridiculed by more sophisticated birds for his clumsiness and lack of social grace.

Even in 19th-century England the matter of owl blindness seemed common belief, for the poet Tennyson in his popular *Idylls Of The King* let a character deride someone as "thrice as blind as any noontide owl."

Owls not only see in broad daylight, they can detect movement more quickly than human eyes do and at a greater distance. In 1942 ornithologist G.L. Walls reported watching a Great Horned Owl react to a hawk approaching high overhead long before he or other humans knew the hawk was anywhere around. Even without such tests, you would conclude that Snowy Owls and Hawk-Owls living in the Far North must have good day vision to survive during the long Arctic summers when there is no night. Farther south, Short-eared Owls also do much of their hunting by day. They may not see as clearly by day as humans do, but they are by no means blind.

However, owls do have difficulty focusing on very small objects, which they normally have no need to see, or on very close objects. To get a better look at something too close for clear image, an owl will move its head (since it cannot move its eyes) bobbing and bowing from side to side, nodding back and forth, lifting its head a bit higher or lowering it—anything to change its own relative position and get a better perception of the puzzle and so decide if action is required. No matter that the reason for this jiggety jerking is sensible. It looks ridiculous—as if the owl is trying to perform some exotic Oriental dance.

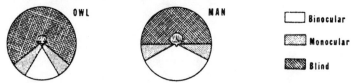

Owls have a narrower range of vision than humans (Oregon Dept. of Fish and Wildlife).

Once you know how firmly owl eyes are fixed in their sockets, of course, you understand. Instead of sliding the eyeball sideways, owls must turn the whole head. Luckily, their neck muscles are extremely flexible and so a mere twitch and the head is halfway around. Another twitch and it could be back to the original position, leaving any watcher who happened to blink at the wrong moment fully convinced an owl can twirl its head all the way around. However, that swivel neck goes just 270° not the full-circle 360°. But some people need a lot of owl-watching before they believe that fact.

All owl species have a third eyelid, a transparent film called a nictitating membrane. This membrane sweeps up to protect the eye from dust and dirt or too bright sunlight. Other birds have this helpful membrane, too, though humans do not.

Although all owl eyes have many features in common, they are not all the same size and do not have the same number of rods and cones. So it seems reasonable to conclude that both daytime and night-time vision vary in quality from one species to another. Many more tests need to be made, but those reported so far indicate that three species—Barred, Long-eared and Common Barn-Owls—may have the keenest dim-light vision. Eye measurements reveal that Eagle Owl, Great Horned, Barred and Snowy—the largest of the owls, but all under three feet in length—have eyes as large as those of human adults. If our eyes were of owl size in comparable proportions, we'd need heads almost the size of washtubs to accommodate them.

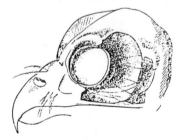

Eye socket of Tawny Owl, Sir William Jardine.

Incidentally, if owl eyes do not look anywhere near as big as your own, remember that only the iris and pupil are visible, with none of the white showing. Remember also, that even though owls can get double light through reflection and re-entrance, they cannot see in total darkness. They have to have some light, however little it may seem to us, as that wise old birdwatcher Pierre Belon proved more than four hundred years ago by isolating an owl in a completely shuttered room. But of course if the eyes can't function, the owls also have ears. And those ears are special.

Ear of Long-eared Owl, John James Audubon.

OWL HEARING IS AMAZING. In some ways, owl ears are even more valuable than owl eyes in overcoming the hazards of nocturnal survival. You can't see them at a glance, for those feather tufts on top of some owl's heads aren't ears, of course. The actual ear openings are well covered by other feathers, however, protecting them from dust and injury. Owl facial muscles can act to spread that feather covering into a directional funnel which directs sound right down to the ear's most sensitive parts. Some owl ears also have a movable flap of skin which forms a reverse funnel to deliver sounds from below the owl's perch up into the ear opening. Owls with tufts may gain additional aid from those feathers as they help deliver surrounding noises to the ears for interpretation and warning. How much the tufts help has not yet been fully tested, but certain experiments suggest that the tufted species have the keenest hearing by day or night, with the Long-eared Owl apparently the most sensitive to sounds.

In most owls each ear is at a different height from the chin, and often of varying shape. These distinctions enable a listening owl to triangulate the exact location of a sound, determining whether it comes from above or below, from what height and distance. All those bristly facial feathers that have added "whiskers" to so many owl names help focus the sound waves, too. They are not there just for adornment. Like almost every other part of owl anatomy, the facial feathers have an important role in improving chances for survival.

Feathers, Sir William Jardine.

FLIGHT FEATHERS WORK LIKE MAGIC. *"Quand il vole, il ne fait aucun bruit!"* Pierre Belon recorded in his remarkable history of birds in 1555. "When it flies it does not make any sound at all!"

That same discovery has been made in awe and wonder by many a birdwatcher since Belon's time, and it is noted in almost every book about owls today. Yet no matter how many times you have read about it, that silent swoop with those amazingly wide wings full spread is a feat you have to see for yourself before you can believe it. Having watched hawks, pheasants, quail, pigeons and so many others in noisy take-off maneuvers, you need explanation of owl silence.

An owl's headfirst thunderbolt plunge from tree branch, barn roof or belfry gives no accompanying roar, not even a rustle of feather against feather to warn the animal crouching below. Darkness hides the plunger and not even a telltale sweep of air stirs until the last minute when the owl suddenly swings its body into a reverse curve with head back, spread talons stretching forward at full reach to make contact with death-grip sureness. Another instant, and the head swings forward again so the hooked beak can sever the vertebrae at the nape for the death-blow. A mercy killing. No catlike playing with a stunned body. No anger involved, only the need to satisfy hunger, the simple matter of one life taken to preserve another. Or several others when there are owlets waiting in the nest hole.

The plunge is noiseless because the outer vane of the two foremost flight feathers forms a loose fringe along the outer edge. Each fluffy fringe-tip is separated from the next in contrast to the tightly-closed edge on the flight feathers of other birds. This loose fluff divides the air currents so they cannot make contact all at once with resulting thump and thud. It preserves silence for all owls except a few species that hunt most often by day when noise is not a factor—Northern Hawk-Owl, the various Pygmy-Owls and Afro-Asian Fishing Owls.

If the silent swoop seems unbelievable to us now, even when we know about the fluffy fringe, imagine how magical it must have seemed to watchers long ago. And there is no doubt they knew this secret of owl success. At least Indians of the Dakota tribes knew, for their word for owl means "Night Bird Who Hunts With Hushed Wings."

☐ *What is the pattern of owl family life?*

Each owl species has its own pattern of mating, nesting and rearing young. However, the Order Strigiformes has more similarities in specific patterns than do most such groups. Some owl species mate for life and most of the others are at least monogamous during the nesting season. Most of them also nest in trees or some other lofty nook, but Snowy Owls and Short-eared Owls nest right on the ground, and the Burrowing Owl prefers an underground tunnel.

Tree nesters usually choose a natural cavity or an abandoned woodpecker hole or they may take over the abandoned nest of a hawk, eagle, crow or raven, without adding much nesting material. If such nests are scarce they may accept a "made-to-order" nest you concoct by piling sticks crisscross on a platform as hawks do or use any convenient cavity in canyon rocks or crumbling walls. In the Old World where tumbled ruins of long-vanished cities are fairly common, owls have come to accept such nooks as suitable quarters. The Little Owl has long been in the habit of choosing such nesting sites and its Arabic name—*'umm al-khirab*—means Mother of the Ruins, Nester Among Ruins.

In addition to choosing a nesting hole, owls must also stake out a hunting territory that they will defend from all intruders. Larger owls need a larger territory than smaller species, and even the smaller ones nesting near cities or other areas where prey is scarce will need more space than those in open country. For example, a Great Horned Owl pair in the East or Midwest claims five to six square miles, but in the Far West open spaces they could eat well with only a one-square-mile claim. The smaller Screech-Owls would need only half as much territory.

Most owls leave a narrow stretch of "No-Owl's-Land" between their claim boundary line and the area of the next owl family. If a neighbor comes too close to the invisible line, a hoot of warning advises it to retreat—and the advice is usually taken. Although every hoot of the same species may sound alike to us, to the owls there's a difference, and the individual can be recognized by its voice. So an owl is seldom in doubt as to whether its mate or a neighbor or a stranger is calling and what the message is.

Courting calls are likely to be the softest, the most musical of all owl sounds. Even the Barn-Owl gives an almost musical *tee-tuh* or *whee-yuh* invitation to a prospective mate. And the Great Horned Owls—who have earned the nickname "Flying Tiger" with their fiercely relentless attacks on foe or food—may act quite dovelike in their courting. The male approaches the female almost timidly, sidling along the branch toward her, bowing and hesitating, ruffling his feathers as if to prove himself all muscle and handsome besides. He may even take a brief circling flight above her and come back for further appeal, perhaps stroke her with his bill, and if she makes no protest they consider themselves pledged and fly off together.

Most male owls make similar overtures as they court a mate. Often they offer a responsive female a bit of food, as if to demonstrate how well they will feed her when she is busy keeping the eggs warm.

When it comes to egg laying, the number runs from two to a dozen, according to species and the availability of food. Female owls will lay fewer eggs than normal or none at all in seasons when their usual food is extremely scarce. Females do most of the incubating or all of it, but even males that do not share the incubating will provide food for mate and young hatchlings. At first the owlets can digest only small pieces of meat, and the male usually lets the female bite off the pieces that match owlet need, but later he will feed the babies himself, at least now and then. The babies may vary markedly in size, for the female usually begins incubation when the first egg is laid and so the chicks hatch on a staggered schedule.

Owlets are born with eyes sealed shut, heads and beaks far too big for their bodies and with little control of their muscles. They flip and flop about and in general look so unappealing that no one would be likely to call them cute. Although their nakedness is soon covered with down amazingly soft to the touch, they still are not in line for a prize in any beauty contest. Compared to baby ducks and chicks and other precocial young ready to run about the moment the birth down dries, owlets wouldn't even be allowed an entry blank. Compared to other altricial young, they're not lacking much more than can be expected. However, that hasn't kept "ugly as a just-hatched owlet" from being a telling phrase.

Certainly the famous French writer of fables, Jean de La Fontaine, thought owlets "grim little monsters. . . . hideous brutes." At least that was how he wrote of them in his tale of the eagle and the owl who pledged never to eat each other's young. Since the owl papa had described his babes as "pretty" and "beautiful . . . well-formed and fine" the eagle who came upon the nest while the parents were both away mistook them for some unknown species and gobbled them up. La Fontaine's moral (for every fable has to have its lesson) is that parents should be more realistic in appraising their offspring. But what parents would believe *they* need such advice? Audubon himself thought young Saw-whets "very neat and beautiful" by the time they took flight. Evidently La Fontaine and others who ridicule owl parents for being overly fond of their young do not realize that young owls—like hawks and other predator species—need more time to learn adult skills than do songbird babies. Songbirds need only fly well enough to catch a few bugs and know how to find berries, seeds, and such easy-pickings. Raptors must know how to hunt and kill, as well as fly, and owls need also to learn the ways of the night. Even owlets hatched in early spring may still need parental guidance through the summer, and a late brood will still be with the parents learning their lessons in the fall. So the word for owl parents could be "protective" or "dutiful" or even "devoted" if you allow a little human feeling to surface. But do not let La Fontaine's fable persuade you they are foolishly fond of their owlets' looks.

☐ *How long do owls live?*

According to Danny Bystrak of the USFWS Bird-Banding Laboratory, so few bands have been returned for most owl species—especially the smaller ones—that their records do not give a satisfactory accounting of owl longevity. Their records are all for wild birds and the oldest owl on tally is a Great Horned Owl at 19 years 3 months. Close behind are a Barred Owl at 18 years 2 months and a Common Barn-Owl at 15 years 5 months. Eastern and Western Screech-Owls have both been reported at around 13 years and a Snowy at 10 years 9 months.

However, a captive Snowy has lived 35 years, a captive Barn-Owl to 51, a Great Gray to 40 and a Great Horned to 38. Undoubtedly life in the wild provides hazards captives do not have to meet and it has been estimated that from 50 to 60 percent of wild hatchlings die during their first year and that few adults make it through ten years.

☐ *Do any tribal legends see owls as portents of good luck?*

AN ANSWER FROM HAWAII:

Only one species of owl is native to the Hawaiian Islands. Because islanders saw it as unique, different from all other birds, it held a special aura of mystery and in olden times they worshipped it as a god. Although it is now called "Hawaiian Owl" by islanders who speak English and *Pu-e-o* by those who use the old language of Hawaii, modern science classifies it as only a geographical race or subspecies of the Short-eared Owl which is known in many other lands.

In recent years the Common Barn-Owl has been introduced on some islands, but *Pu-e-o* is still "the" owl for most Hawaiians even though it is now extremely scarce. Compare it to Short-eared Owls elsewhere and you will see little difference except its slightly darker plumage. Like all of its species it is silent most of the year and a sort of muffled doglike *wow-wow* is almost the only comment you're likely to hear. However, in courting time it offers a series of musical, low-pitched *toot-toot* or *coo-coo* notes that could easily have sounded like *pu-pu* to listening Hawaiians of long ago and so led to *pu-e-o* name in the days when legends such as the following were first told:

KAPOI AND THE OWL GOD. *Long, long ago when people and birds and all the other animals shared the same world and all knew each other's speech and ways, a certain poor fisherman named Kapoi lived in a humble grass-roofed hut near what is now Honolulu's Punch Bowl Hill. Things had not been going well for Kapoi. For one thing, his roof had been pelted by so much rain that it was now just slimy clumps instead of tidily over-lapping layers of pili grass. And the plants in his taro patch had either molded or floated away. And for days he had not caught a single fish, so he was not only wet and cold in his little hut but hungry, too.*

Still, the only food he could hope for was fish, and so on this morning he once again set out with his nets. Once

*again he tossed them out with care and once again they
came back empty. "Well," he told himself. "If I can't eat,
I can at least mend my roof and be warm and dry." So off
he went to look for the tall and sturdy pili grass that
makes the best thatch and soon found all he wanted.*

*"Maybe my luck is changing," he thought as he shoul-
dered the bundles of grass and headed for home. And
changed it was, for all at once he looked down to make
sure of his footing and there was a pu-e-o nest right there
on the ground in front of him, almost hidden by the usual
clump of grasses that provides windbreak and camouflage. In the nest hollow—his for the taking—were seven
owl eggs with neither he-owl nor she-owl on guard.
Quickly he scooped them up, his stomach already rum-
bling in anticipation of owl-egg supper, and headed for
home as fast as he could go with his double burden,
scarcely believing good fortune could have come so
unexpectedly.*

*He had his cookfire going in no time, the flames licking
at the oven stones in his baking pit, heating them nicely.
Next he gathered fresh ti leaves, enough to wrap each egg
twice over so that it would not cook too fast or burn. Now
he began the wrapping, taking time to do it just right, and
putting each wrapped egg beside the others, all in a row,
waiting and ready. He was just reaching for the last egg
when he heard a strange voice calling in anguished tones
from somewhere overhead.*

*"Kapoi! Oh, Kapoi!" came the quavery call, and Kapoi
looked up to see an owl on his rooftop, wings wide-spread
and feathers flaring, yellow eyes ablaze in anger.*

*"You took my eggs! You took my eggs!" shrieked the
owl. "All of them. Every one. Thief! Thief!"*

*Kapoi cringed. He knew he had been wrong to take all
the eggs, leaving none for the owls to hatch. But at the
time he had been too bemused by sudden fortune to think
of right and wrong. And too hungry.*

"How many do you want back?" he asked grudgingly.

"Seven!" hissed the owl. "Seven my mate laid and seven

71

we want returned to us. Right now—before they get cold and will not hatch."

"But I'm hungry," Kopoi protested. "I haven't eaten since——"

"Eggs are more to us than food! They are our children-to-be. Give them back!"

Kapoi tried to pretend he hadn't understood a single word and started to lay the first egg on the hot stones. His stomach told him that was the right thing to do, but his heart couldn't help thinking of how much children mean, even to owls.

"Take your eggs," he told Pueo gruffly, and went into the hut and shut the door behind him. He could hear Pueo and his mate talking together as they carried away the eggs, but he did not look out to watch them. Finally when all was silent, he went out to tend to his fire and suddenly Pueo appeared out of the dusk.

"Oh, Kapoi," he said in kindly tone. "You have done a difficult thing. You have put others ahead of yourself. Now if you will accept me as your personal god, build me a temple there on the hill and worship me as a god should be worshipped, I will protect you from evil forever more, and if you have need, all the owls of all the islands will come to your aid."

Kapoi was glad to accept, for refusal would surely have brought misfortune. It was island custom for each man to choose his own gods as he pleased, so long as he continued to respect the gods chosen by the king and did not interfere with any taboos the king imposed. So he built the temple, and all began to go well for him.

But then the king heard about the new owl-god temple and declared that Kapoi had violated the rights of the royal gods and so must pay for this crime with his life. No sooner did the king's soldiers read this verdict to him than they bound Kapoi hand and foot and hustled him off down the hill to the palace dungeon on Waikiki Beach.

There he must wait till plans for beheading him were complete.

Kapoi had no chance to send his owl-god a message, but of course the god soon heard what had happened. At once he went to the King Of Owls who lived in Manoa Valley on Owl Hill and asked that his pledge to Kapoi be fulfilled. And at once the Owl King sent word for all owls from all islands to come and take vengeance as promised. In a trice every owl on every island took to the air. On they came, from all directions, uniting in one vast, dark-winged cloud over the dungeon courtyard at Waikiki Beach where soldiers, priests, nobles and peasants were gathering as commanded by their king to witness the beheading. Just as the soldiers brought Kapoi up for execution the great, wide-winged birds came swooping down, talons reaching out to slash whatever human flesh they encountered. Swoop, slash, swoop and slash again! Just as the swooping, slashing mass was about to reach the king himself, the monarch cried out in surrender, promising Kapoi would go free and his owl-god would be held sacred forever more.

The promise was kept. Kapoi lived in plenty all his days and the owl-god was worshipped as a god should be and the site of the battle became a sacred place, too. Kuka-e-un-ahio-ka-pueo, it was called, and some still remember the place and the name: Place of the confused noise of owls flying in masses.

AS IT COULD HAVE HAPPENED:

Everyone who studies old legends and folk tales soon learns that even some of the most unlikely ones have at least a small morsel of fact working like yeast in bread dough to evoke the fantasy. The morsel is in Kapoi's story, all right, though well camouflaged.

Throughout history there have been several proved occurrences of birds of prey—owls, gulls, hawks—suddenly appearing in large numbers in unexpected places at the very moment the area was being plagued with hordes of mice, rats, locusts, grasshoppers or other pests. The birds destroy the invading pests and then disperse to their accustomed routes, usually leaving behind many a farmer who suddenly sees the value of these raptors in human economics.

Such flights of owl pest-control service were recorded in Europe in the 1600s and in South America in the 1870s. Probably the best-known North American incident occurred in 1848 when gulls swarmed into Utah from all directions to devour the grasshoppers that were destroying the pioneer settlers' crops. No mention of insects or rodents is involved in the Hawaiian legend—perhaps because no one had been close enough to realize the real reason for the sudden descent of avenging predators. But the "confused noises" and the "flying masses" could have been heard and seen and wondered about earnestly enough for someone to feel the need to create a story to explain all.

Another legend of the owl-god of Manoa Valley on Oahu tells how this wonder-worker saved the life of a beautiful valley maiden three times, on each occasion rescuing her from an evil warrior who forced her to live with him against her will. After the third rescue she was so weary and heartsick that she could do nothing but weep and moan and no longer had any desire to live. So the owl-god turned her tears into a beautiful waterfall and let her go to the spirit world where no human could reach her ever again.

ANOTHER ANSWER FROM ANCIENT TARTARY:

For the Tartars, the Barn-Owl has long been honored as one who brought life, not death, and the change all came about this way:

Early in the 13th century the great Tartar prince Genghis

74

Khan had just finished his conquest of Mongolia and was now leading his armies southward into China, dividing his troops to raid first here, then elsewhere, in surprise attacks.

By the year 1215 he would have most of China in his power, and even other lands farther southward, but he did not win every battle along the way. Indeed, one night he came close to losing everything he had gained just because he and the small band of raiders with him had been too exhausted to take full precaution against pursuit before they bedded down for the night.

Luckily, one man was still alert enough to make midnight reconnaissance, and he came racing back to rouse the camp with shouts of warning. Somehow the enemy they thought soundly beaten had rallied in pursuit and would be on them in moments, well-armed and ready for vengeance.

No time to draw up battle lines. No time for anything but to grab their weapons and run, each man for himself.

"Meet at headquarters," the prince ordered tersely, and then was off into the woods like his men, trying to blend with the shadows, slip from one patch of cover to the next, hoping he could get far enough ahead so that he could return to the trail. But of course he couldn't. Those who were after him already had their "night eyes" and were on familiar terrain besides. Soon he could hear them close behind him—had guessed they would hear his every move, too, any moment now. One chance to fool them— and he took it, squirming as noiselessly as possible into the very center of a thick and thorny clump of underbrush, holding his breath as he lowered himself full length, flat against the ground. He was no sooner stretched out and daring to breathe again than he felt something rustle the branches overhead and looked up, expecting to see a gloating enemy face, and instead met the calm dark-eyed gaze of a golden-coated owl. The prince held himself as motionless as he could manage and the owl held its place, *motionless, too, as if it were on some warpath of its own. Even when two of the pursuing enemy soldiers came creeping through the brush, the owl still sat there, perhaps guessing from their movements that they were not on owl hunt this time.*

They saw the owl, looked at each other and shrugged. "So he didn't come this way," one said, "or that owl wouldn't still be sitting there. Come on." And off they went in another direction.

When there was no longer even the faintest whisper of their footsteps, the owl suddenly spread its wings and left also. The prince sent a silent message of thanks for its protection in his moment of need and promised on his honor that all of his people would give homage to owls with the golden coat.

And so they did, once they heard his tale. For all the years Genghis Khan lived and ruled, and even for many a year thereafter, all of Tartar blood and loyalty gave their Golden Owl—or White Owl as some called it because of its white face and breast—due homage. It became the custom for Tartars to show their loyalty by wearing an owl feather in their headdresses, especially at festivals or on other special occasions. Some even carried a little carved figure of the owl as mascot and good-luck charm.

If any of Tartar descent still pay the Barn-Owl this traditional homage, they may well have forgotten the reason for it after so many centuries. But even in the 1700s many knew the story of the prince and his owl and told it to any European travelers who came to their land.

However, certain travelers who returned from those same countries insisted they'd heard it was a wild peacock, not a mere owl, who had saved the prince. Perhaps he had to hide on more than one occasion. Or perhaps somebody thought peacock feathers were handsomer than owl plumes and changed the story to match. At any rate, the Barn-Owls had several centuries of honor in Tartar lands to offset at least a little the stigma of death and ill omen that follows them almost everywhere else.

☐ *Have writers ever described owl call-notes as music?*

In the year 1110 when the great Canterbury cathedral was being built, stone carvers were employed to decorate the pillars with appropriate designs and figures. Of course music is at the heart of every church service, and so one carver chose to encircle his pillar-heading with a quartet of musicians, each with his instrument.

For some reason—possibly because he thought there were too many saints and angels on the other pillars and he liked to be different—his four musicians were animals. An eagle-headed lion twanged on a harp, a greyhound had his lips to some kind of flute, a goat had that ancient reed instrument now known as oboe, and the last figure held a violin-shaped instrument and a bow. Not much argument about what he was playing, but those who come now to see the Pillar of the Musicians are usually ready to argue over whether this last music-maker is an owl—as wings and hornlike tufts seem to prove—or the devil himself.

Since the other three are undoubtedly animals, it seems reasonable to give fourth place to the owl, especially since the wings look feathered. Because of the horns, the artist most likely had the Eagle Owl in mind. And it is possible he was trying to put on record that he thought violin music as screechy as owl hootings, not owl calls as musical as the lilting strains of a well-played violin. However, then as now, the difference between screeching and music must surely lie in the ear of the listener.

ALSO FROM ENGLAND, 16TH TO 20TH CENTURIES:

William Shakespeare himself gave the call of the Tawny Owl a vote of approval. And although he did not exactly go so far as to label it music, he did write of its "merry note" in *Love's Labour Lost*, Act V, Scene II, in what he called his "Winter Song" almost at play's end.

Furthermore, he translated that merriness to English syllables as *tu-who, tu-whit, tu-who,* and endless writers ever since have accepted those sounds as the one and only perfect match for owl serenade, regardless of which species is singing. Even well into the 19th century Tennyson was borrowing Shakespeare's coinage for owl conversation—and complaining that he couldn't imitate it with anything like exactness, which may have been a hint he thought Avon's bard had missed exactness also.

In some of Shakespeare's other plays his ear did not report merriment in owl voices. His night birds shriek in *MacBeth* and clamor in *Midsummer Night's Dream,* and elsewhere in *MacBeth* toll the death knell. Nevertheless, the British co-authors of Roger Tory Peterson wrote of "musical" notes for Tengmalm's Owl (Boreal Owl on U.S. lists) as well as for the Tawny, even though the syllables for Tawny talk were *hoo-hoo-hoo, oo-oo-oo-oo.* As Tennyson put it, "Not a whit of thy tu-whoo." Anyone who wants to add his own comment must do his own listening, either to the owls themselves or to a good recording.

FROM THE UNITED STATES, 19TH AND 20TH CENTURIES:

Thoreau heard owl voices at evening beside Walden Pond and labeled them ghostly wailing—and liked them that way. "I rejoice that there are owls," he wrote, evidently because the eerie voices were so well suited to swamps and twilight woods and to the yearnings of unsatisfied humans who surely never have the voice to express their disappointments so fittingly. The key to

78

thinking owl cries melodious is evidently to listen in such melancholy surroundings—and especially from a distance. Twentieth century writers suggest that the only musical owl calls are those of courting season—another notch in the owl musical key.

☐ *What part do owls play in ancient Jewish writings and early Christian lore?*

In Leviticus and Deuteronomy when the birds unfit for human food are listed, owls are named along with daytime predators. Just how many owl species are on the roster is disputed by translators, for some of the names are no longer used and their meaning is uncertain. Whatever the names, all owls were included because all feed on bloody prey and most of them also on carrion, if fresh-killed animals are not available. Two names, however, are generally accepted: *kos*, the Little Owl (a word echoic of its cough-like call) and *yanshuf*, "the horned one," for the Eagle Owl. If the name in between these two—*shalak*, the "plunger"—identifies the Tawny Owl, which does indeed "plunge" into the meadow grasses after mice, then you have a trio which could also ban all small, medium-sized and large owls. A fourth name *tinshemeth*, the "hisser" may give special banning to the Barn-Owl.

Elsewhere, however, the Barn-Owl is given the name of *lilith*, "night hag, night monster." Along with all other references to owls in the Hebrew Scriptures or the Old Testament of Christian Bibles, *lilith* is named to emphasize a scene of doom and desolation where only the wildest of wildlings could survive. "A place for owls" as pictured by Isaiah and Zephaniah includes no amenities whatsoever.

No owls are mentioned in New Testament passages, although they are no doubt included by implication in the reference to "unclean birds" in Revelation. But in the Middle Ages, as the story of Christianity became well accepted throughout Europe, owls were sometimes given a role in folk tales. By the time the Renaissance was making Christian themes almost a "must" for successful artists, many a painter was adding an owl to scenes of Calvary or any other setting in which death could be foretold.

Christian belief now held that Christ's death on the cross had been ordained from his birth. So in the 16th century when Juan de Flandes painted his scene of Bethlehem stable, he added the omen no one of his time would miss—a Barn-Owl, looking down with wise-eyed solemnity upon the Babe and his Mother.

In this same era, storytellers in Spain reminded the children that owls once had a beautiful voice, sweet and melodious. But when an owl at Calvary saw the dying Savior, it called out *Cruz! Cruz!* bemoaning that such an instrument of torture as a cross should be used, and kept calling that one word so long its voice lost all its sweetness. From then on it could only moan and mourn, as all owls have done ever since.

Better known, at least in England, is the tale Shakespeare had in mind in 1602 or thereabout as he let Ophelia make cryptic answer to the king's simple greeting of "How do you, pretty lady?" with these words: "Well, God 'ild [yield] you! They say the owl was a baker's daughter. Lord, we know what we are, but know not what we may be."

Probably everyone in Shakespeare's audiences knew the tale of how the Lord Jesus came to a bakeshop one day in poor man's disguise and asked for the mercy of a loaf of bread. Grudgingly, the baker's daughter pinched off as small a piece of dough as she dared and put it in the oven to bake. When it somehow grew to twice size, she was about to pinch off an even stingier piece when she was suddenly changed into an owl and flew off huffing and hooting in dismay.

When Swedish grandmothers told this tale, the girl was

changed into a woodpecker. In Germany the miserly one was a baker's boy who became a cuckoo. In Greece a servant became an owl after trying to steal a dress intended for the statue of the virgin, so the owls had the worst of it in these legends as in many others.

☐ *When is an owl not an owl?*

When do you talk of owls and not mean owls at all? Usually when you need a metaphor for human night-time behavior. "What a night owl!" you growl when your neighbor's garage door creaks and squeaks to waken you at three a.m.—again.

Suburban parents giving last-minute advice to a teen-ager about to spend a first solo spree in the city are likely to come out with stern reminder the "owl car" leaves the downtown train station at one-thirty sharp.

Anywhere, anytime, anyone with overly solemn mien is likely to be tagged an owl, too. And since so many of us resent people who know more than we do—or act as if they do—being classed with the owls may have a decidedly uncomplimentary overtone. "What does Professor Owl say now?" someone may ask with sneer or smirk. English author Thomas Carlyle once gave put-down tag to one overly-erudite lecture as "owl-eyed pedantry" and no one mistook it for praise.

In Italy, so owl-watcher Eugenio Gavioli of Milan reports, the Eagle Owl used to wear the aura of wisdom first claimed by Athena's Little Owl companion. But in recent years the big owl has been the symbol of disaster in so many horror movies that to call someone *gufo* (the Italian echo of *bubo* call notes) now pictures a person of gloom and dark despair and aloof withdrawal.

And instead of being a bird of wisdom, the Tawny Owl (most abundant of Italian owl species) is a ready Italian idiom for stupidity. *"Con la faccia di un allocco,"* Italians

81

say with a shrug, making "owl face" the equivalent of a dunce cap.

Well, then, so there are owls—and owls. And always have been, according to the way we humans see them. A century ago the comment that you'd been seen "owling" usually meant you were gazing at the moon and sighing over a sweetheart not yet won, or at least looking as if you were indulging in romantic dreams of some kind. But two centuries ago, in England, the meaning would have been quite different. Owlers in those times were smugglers, sneaking in a cargo of contraband French gloves or lace or fine brandy by dark of night while most folk closed their shutters tight and counted the money they'd save if they could buy these wares without the high tax proper storekeepers had to charge.

These days—or nights—the owler term is for those of us who go out with binoculars and bird guides, hoping to see an owl species we haven't seen before or to get a better look at those we already have entered on our list. If we glance over the shoulder at a sudden leaf rustle or the snap of a twig on the path behind us, it's neither with dread of a sheriff's posse or hope of a sweetheart. What we want is another look to see if that owl head was rounded or tufted, if the eyes were yellow or black, or any other clue to prove identity.

And so it goes for owlers and for owls.

6

OWLS FACE A
THREATENING WORLD

WHAT NEXT FOR THE SPOTTED OWL?

IN WESTERN WOODLANDS from British Columbia to
Baja California lives an owl that hears the same death-
warning in the whine of a logger's chain-saw that primitive humans have read in an owl's moan and banshee
wail. For the Spotted Owl this is no imaginary threat. It is
real, beyond doubt. The only debatable point is how close
the species is to extinction and when—if ever—the threat
will loom beyond human control.

Because these birds are shy and seldom stray far from
deep forest sanctuary, the species was not classified for
scientific record until 1859—17th of the 19 North American owls to go on official record. Its classifier was an
enterprising Hungarian naturalist, Janos Xántus, who

also used the surname De Vesey. Exiled as a revolutionist from his native land, he became an eager western pioneer and also served Army duty at Fort Tejon, California, where he put this owl on the book as *Syrnium occidentale,* meaning "Western Bird of Ill Omen." The name has now been revised to *Strix occidentalis,* which labels it "Western Night Hag" or simply "Western Owl," depending on how you translate that ancient term *strix.* Like all other species in this genus it has a round head with no ear tufts and with no pointed chin to give it a heart-shaped face.

Spotted Owl,
Encyclopedia Britannica, 1910.

As for its common name, its breast and belly do seem to be spotted rather than streaked or barred. and if you look at it side by side with its eastern relative the Barred Owl, *Strix varia,* you can tell the difference. However, you're more likely to see the two separately rather than together, so you need to study the pictures in the guide books to be sure which you're seeing these days, for Barred Owls have been moving west, especially through Canada, and are even invading some of the Spotted Owl territory where *varia* were never seen before. The Barred Owl is slightly larger, but not much, and the two rank fourth and fifth among North America's largest owls. Both wear a gray-brown-white blending of spots, bars, streaks and flecks that provide excellent camouflage as they huddle up against a tree trunk for daytime napping.

The Spotted Owl is the only one of the two threatened with extinction and it is endangered for several reasons. First, it has never been an abundant and wide-ranging species able to re-coup losses in one area with good reproduction elsewhere. It is found in older forest areas only—and only in the West—and so destruction of that habitat is tantamount to elimination of the species. Also it usually lays only two eggs—occasionally three and even less often four—and seldom attempts a second brood if the first is destroyed by climate or predators.

It has never been exceptionally successful in self-defense and is often the prey of Great Horned Owls. Lately, invading Barred Owls have also taken toll by preempting nesting sites and by predation. But the loggers are the main threat. Old-growth timber is getting in shorter and shorter supply every year and there doesn't seem to be enough left even now for both the owls and the loggers to have all they need. Or at least all they want.

The favorite areas for both are stands of conifers, for the most part, especially Douglas firs some 400-750 years old. Only here can the owls find the large trees with broken tops and cavities they are programmed by nature to choose as nesting sites, lookout posts and roosting platforms. The same forest provides the loggers with good income, but once trees are cut another 40 or 50 years must pass before new seedlings can grow to anything even approaching Spotted Owl requirement—and the species can't wait that long without being replenished by the usual yearly crop of owlets. A captive Spotted Owl has been known to live 21 years, but without records from wild birds we can only guess they reach 12 or 15 at best and will average much less for the entire population, no doubt, if a complete census could be taken.

Of course loggers will say quite honestly that they can't go without income any more than owls can survive as a species without offspring. Somehow a fair decision has to be made with concern for both people and owls—and all the other wildlife that uses the old-growth forest as home. In fall 1988, the Forest Service intends to approve a ban on logging in 347,000 of the 1.3 million acres of old-growth forest in Washington and Oregon. The plan is aimed at protecting the Spotted Owl and other wildlife. However, it has drawn sharp criticism from the timber interests and as of publication of this book has not yet been signed by Forest Service officials.

Unfortunately, the owls can't express their preferences—except by not nesting at all if they can't find the kind of site they are accustomed to use. Will they be adaptable enough to use manmade nest boxes or other sites when the old-growth trees are gone? They do sometimes nest in rocky crevices—but there aren't too many of those around, either. At least not in the lonely woodlands that Spotted Owls have long considered the only safe place to raise a family. And if they ever do get used to different nesting accommodations, will there be enough individuals left to maintain a species?

If not—how and when and where will the last Spotted Owl left on earth vanish forever? Will it take its last breath within the bars of a zoo cage like the last Passenger Pigeon—with some human standing by watch in hand to record the last day, month, year and the ultimate and unalterable tick of the clock? Or will it disappear unmarked by human eyes at all, like the last Ivory-billed Woodpecker, leaving hopeful humans to keep searching, searching—and condemning themselves for not having realized the danger sooner and made greater effort at rescue?

All the federal agencies in control of land where Spotted Owls now nest—U.S. Forest Service, Bureau of Land Management, National Parks—have made some studies. So have some state agencies and a few concerned private groups involved in wildlife conservation and even a few individual owl-watchers. One such entrepreneur, Jerry Mires of Umpqua County, Oregon, has devised an original method for tracking each Spotty to its hard-to-find nest-hole. The bait is a fresh caught mouse hooked into a fishline ready to be reeled out as the owl makes off with mouse firmly clenched in beak. As the owl heads for its nest where hungry nestlings wait with open beaks and squawking pleas, the line trails through the trees behind. Without the fishline, the trail could easily be lost, and sometimes even with it, for the line can easily be caught in a tangle while the owl makes off with half a mouse or none. But at least somebody, even several somebodies, are out there trying.

Meanwhile, though no other North American owl species is yet in danger of extinction, a few individuals are at the mercy of humans who think any large bird—especially any predator--is fair game, in spite of laws to the contrary. And when one of those owls—trapped, shot, poisoned—happens to be one some fond owl-watcher has seen grow from owlet to adult right in her own back-yard—well, the loss is not easy to take. At least that's how the author felt when her own owlet neighbor met its untimely end.

SOME HUMANS HARM.

We didn't name him. He wasn't a pet, just a wildling neighbor, and already on his own, as is the way of the owl clan. It had been March or April, I think, when children passing by on the way to school stopped to tell us that funny-looking little fuzz-ball owlets were hatching in the old woodpecker's hole in a wind-topped Douglas fir up on the hill.

Now and then through the early summer evenings I had caught a glimpse of the parents and heard their tremulous calls, so I knew that these were Screech-Owls. Western Screech-Owls, of course, since our hillside is in Oregon. By early August the young were on their own and one of them chose our yard and the hillside stretching beyond through blackberry tangles for his private mousehunting preserve. He was good at his job, too. For soon there were fewer and fewer field mice, shrews and voles coming down to raid the feeding tables we put out for birds, squirrels, chipmunks and raccoons.

I was having a good many sleepless nights that year, a few too many aches and pains for comfort, and it was good to lie there in the dark and listen to Owlet's "hoo-hooing," a little quavery serenade coming out of the night stillness. Sometimes he was in the trees at the back, but more often he was on the utility pole at the front where he had a good chance to snack on any moth or night-flying insect attracted by the street light. Large insects are almost as important an item on the Screech-Owl menu as rodents. And of course the smaller birds would be fair prey for him, too, now that he was full size. As he himself was fair prey for larger predators in Nature's inevitable scheme of check-and-balance.

Adult owls are usually silent as they hunt, but our Owlet liked the sound of his voice. "Woo-oo, wu-wu-wu, woo-oo!" he seemed to stutter, as if he could not quite get out the syllables in proper flow. It would be a spooky call to hear if you were all alone in the woods, but when you're safe in your own bed it seems more like a telegrapher's key tapping out the message for any anti-mice humans that the nightly hunt is under control and they can go back to sleep with mind assured.

But Owlet will not be calling outside my window again. One morning my husband found him lying on the grass beneath his favorite perch, eyes shut in death, head hunched down on his shoulders as if he'd sat there feeling the poison working within him, feeling it take over muscle by muscle until at last he could sit upright no longer and just toppled over. Somewhere in backyards nearby he must have eaten mice that had been poisoned, or perhaps had eaten the poison itself, hidden in meat put out by people who did not stop to think that their hidden death lure might be found by someone other than the rodents they meant to destroy.

Instead of Owlet the bait could have been eaten by a pet dog or cat, a friendly squirrel, jays, birds of several kinds. But it was found by Owlet and we miss him. And on following nights when I lay awake listening in vain for his little stuttery notes, I wished then—and still wish—I could find a way to make more people understand the role each living creature holds in nature's interlocking plan.

Snowy Owl, Wes Guderian.

SOME HUMANS LEND A HAND.

The Snowy Owl that came on lame-wing waver across the Columbia River into Oregon that November day in 1977 was on all counts a stranger in a strange land. The Snowy is one species that can survive on frozen tundra year round most years, since their prey, the lemmings, hares and few other species survive, too. But if disaster strikes the rodent population, the Snowy is in trouble, and then the big white birds begin to drift southward for winter forage and will not return until February or early March.

This wanderer must have been close to starving before it left its northern homeland, and now that lame left wing kept it from hunting even in this land of plenty. Somehow it managed to get across the river before collapsing on the far bank, unable to muster enough strength to go on to the beckoning flatland around the Troutdale airport, just a little way beyond, where mice could surely be found.

It would have died from exhaustion and hunger—or become a meal for another predator—except for a lucky break. Workmen were operating a dredge just a short way down river, and by chance one of them spotted it. Maybe nine men out of ten would have kicked the limp bird over and gone back to the dredge in disgust, but this was the Tenth Man. He liked birds and knew the Portland Audubon Society had started a rehabilitation program for wounded birds and other wildlife. So he picked it up carefully and called the Society for advice.

No trouble wrapping the Snowy in a length of sacking. It was too exhausted, too much in shock to notice. And soon Dr. Peter Davis, the volunteer vet on call, was checking x-rays, finding no broken bones, only severe wing sprain. The bird had probably crashed into hard-to-see power lines it had never learned to avoid on the wire-free tundra.

"Weight about three pounds," Davis entered on the chart. The bird could gain a good ten pounds and still not be over-weight. What it needed most was food. A mouse was placed beneath the Snowy's beak—and accepted, gulped down whole, owl fashion, with bones and fur to be regurgitated later in a tidy pellet.

If the Rehab Center had been finished then, the next step would have put the Snowy in a big cage where it could stay safely till the wing healed. But nothing like that was ready and so Dr. Davis volunteered his family as owl-sitters over the next weeks. They'd taken a similar job with pleasure a couple of years before when a 2-month-old orphan Great Horned Owl needed sponsoring until it was ready to be on its own. They had also helped a Red-tailed Hawk that had lost a wing to gunshot wounds. Two peacocks, 15 guinea hens, 20 graylag geese and assorted sheep, rabbits, ducks and chickens were also in the Davis menage, along with two dogs who considered themselves family. The Snowy was welcome and the same spare bathroom that had made temporary quarters for the Great Horned Owlet was now Snowy domain. A five-foot step ladder offered a perch when he felt ready to try his wings.

Snowy was relishing every mouse, shrew, vole and other items offered these days and abundant food made all the difference. No sign of shock or weakness now and apparently no dismay at being an owl in human territory. It was his territory, too, and his acceptance of the unfamiliar is a tribute to the Davises—and perhaps to Snowy wisdom. He had found out what it was like to be at starvation's edge and not once did he nip a hand that fed him.

Snowy Owl, Wes Guderian.

By Christmas he was reaching his ladder with some ease and in early January Mrs. Davis decided he needed more flying space before being released. She invited him into the family room and he accepted, gave it brief survey and reacted like a kid turned loose in a toy store. On his southbound wanderings he had probably perched on shed rooftops, haystacks, stumps or fenceposts and the family room offered a similar variety of shapes and heights. He tried the ironingboard for first landing. Next came the top of the bookcase. Then the upper bar of Mrs. Davis's loom. When he soared over to the top of the freezer without the least wing wobble, everybody was ready to applaud but didn't, lest the clapping seem threat instead of approval.

"Tchk-tchk," Snowy remarked conversationally, as he did now and then when things were going to suit him.

"He's ready to leave us," Ursula Davis said. "You know we have to let him go."

The family knew. They had kept the Horned Owl orphan so long it felt more at ease with humans than in the wild. After a few weeks on its own it had come back, spied Dr. Davis in the garden and came swooping down to his feet, pretending to wrestle with a corner of his trouser cuff as it had done for feed-me signal in babyhood. From then on it had lived outdoors in a convenient tree hollow but came to the yard to be fed often. Eventually contact with a live power wire ended its life, and the "let-wildlings-stay-wild" lesson it had taught remained with the Davises.

In preparation for release an ornithologist with banding permit gave Snowy leg band Number 608-37014 to identify him if he were re-taken. If his captor knew the band's meaning, it would be sent to the Office of Migratory Bird Management, U.S. Fish & Wildlife Service, Laurel, MD 20708, but as of May 1988 no report would come. By New Year's Day Snowy was ready for take-off but Dr. Davis decided to wait a few days till after duck-hunting season was over lest some careless gunner end Snowy's homeward venture before it began.

By this time a number of articles about the Snowy had

appeared in Portland newspapers and on TV news reports. So on January 17, 1978, when Dr. Davis readied his winged visitor for farewell flight there was quite an audience of photographers, reporters and well-wishers on hand. The take-off site was carefully chosen—open grassland for wing room but trees and underbrush nearby if the bird became frightened and needed easy refuge.

No such precaution was needed. Snowy took to freedom as nonchalantly as he had accepted his weeks of recovery and confinement. One moment to take his bearings, and off he went. Watchers had time only to gasp in wonder that those white wings were so wide, for owl wings are wider than other birds of similar body size, and then he was gone.

Those of us who saw him go, either there on Sauvie Island grassland or on TV, will always have a special memory niche for Snowy. And when we read that Micmac Indians of Newfoundland used to say that the Snowy's quavery *koo-koo-shoo* call is a lament that owls and humans are no longer friends and neighbors as they used to be in olden days when the world was young, with each accepting and understanding the others' ways, we can't help thinking that perhaps, just for a few weeks, the old innocence and trust had been shared by bird and mortals once again.

Much the same feeling must have come to owl-watchers in Richland County, South Carolina, in the fall of 1986 when another wandering Snowy offset its bewilderment at being so far from home with unusual acceptance of friendship offered by delighted humans. For a whole week it held court, happily chasing live mice released by equally happy South Carolinians, most of whom had never seen a wild Snowy before although wanderers had reached the state occasionally since Audubon's day at least. However, one watcher felt the bird was too tame and trusting for its own good and turned it over to the Riverbanks Zoo in Columbia. Zoo authorities, mindful of federal regulations banning the capture of wild birds, sent it to the Raptor Rehabilitation Center in Minnesota. Eventually it was released and the rest of its story has not yet been told.

Their action is reminder that adopting any wild bird or caging it in any way is forbidden by national and state laws within the United States, and the ban is supported by Canada, Mexico and the USSR, at least for some migrant species that share their lands as well as ours. Even taking a wounded bird is illegal, except for emergency treatment, and the bird must then be released as soon as it is able to survive in the wild or be taken to the nearest rehabilitation center approved by the U.S. Fish and Wildlife Service.

Severely wounded owls—with an amputated wing perhaps or similar injury—are often kept at rehab centers and become quite tame. They recognize their keepers or others who feed them and often behave with charming aplomb when taken to visit schools or club meetings, thereby converting many a non-birder to an instant owl admirer. But there are also owls that never adjust to crippling wounds or caging, even with the bounty of unfailing food supply.

Caring for just-hatched orphan birds poses special problems, for many newborns tend to accept as parent and role model the first larger creature who pays them attention. Their minds are imprinted with the image of this individual as the one to follow and imitate and they may never learn to accept one of their own species as parent or mate or companion.

Professional attendants at zoos and rehabilitation centers have learned to feed such orphans while wearing a puppet "glove" in the shape of the proper parent's head and beak. That's not too difficult, but trying to look and act like an owl (or whatever) while teaching the adoptee to hunt for its food, to fly, to court a mate takes more trouble than most of us can handle. It also denies the orphan its normal life, and so state and federal laws have been passed to help us all do what is best for the birds even if we are denied the thrill of winning a wildling's trust and friendship.

If that's still a role you crave, volunteer at the nearest rehabilitation center. You may have to begin with the job of cleaning cages or storing mice in the freezer, but happier chores will come in time. And when you are there to see a recovered patient take to wild wing—and know you have helped—you'll not doubt it was worth whatever you had to give.

7
Owl Pharmacopia

WOULD YOU BELIEVE that a concoction of owl eyeballs, carefully charred at fire's edge and then dried and powdered, was a treatment for failing eyesight your European ancestors might have used only four or five generations ago? Would you believe that ancestors on every other continent would have understood the principle behind the prescription and perhaps have had a similar dosage in their own copybook of home remedies?

The reasoning behind almost worldwide belief in such medication is elementary. In ancient times most people believed that illness was somehow paired with magic and might therefore be cured with some sort of matching witchcraft in return. If you had liver trouble, for instance, the best match was to try healing it with a potion or poultice made from the liver of some animal or leaves of liver shape. And if your eyes were the problem, then the eyes of the owl, the creature with the most remarkable vision in the entire Animal Kingdom, would surely help.

Even owl feathers might have value, according to the Cherokee Indians of eastern North America. Their remedy called for steeping the feathers in warm water or letting them simmer over a low fire for a time and then bathing the eyes with the resultant broth. Even a child could stay awake all night after such treatment.

In Morocco in olden days wearing a carefully preserved owl eyeball on a thong around the neck was thought to ward off evil of any kind. In ancient India a concoction brewed from owl eyeballs was considered a cure for children subject to fits and seizures. Add a bit of owl brain to the brew for even surer success, especially if the patient were a woman in labor. Also a soup of owl meat and bones cooked slowly till the liquid jelled was said to provide an excellent salve for soothing the aches of rheumatic joints. And feeding a child some of the fat skimmed from the broth would help guard it from misfortunes of every kind.

The Roman naturalist Pliny suggested a poultice of owl flesh was helpful in relieving the sting of insect bites. Owl soup was useful in easing epileptic seizures. And those of greater faith—but lesser fondness for owl taste on the tongue—claimed just drawing the likeness of an owl eye and having it handy would ward off those unnameable evils always in the air.

In Yorkshire, England, in the Middle Ages—and even later—one mother would tell another that a cup or two of good warm owl broth would ease a child through whooping cough or even prevent it altogether. Old-time German household remedies for the bite of a mad dog—or at least the prevention of such misfortune—was to carry the heart of an owl and its right foot under one's armpit. Good health would surely bless a child who slept in a cradle adorned by an entire stuffed owl, in case you couldn't persuade a live one to make it a regular perching place. Even a dried owl's foot might help.

In central Europe many believed that a soldier who

carried an owl's heart into battle would surely fight with outstanding bravery.

And since owls were so full of wisdom, they were also thought of value in aiding an alcoholic to give up his drinking habits. The English recipe for such service was not easy, however. You had to eat owl eggs—whole and raw— gulped down as fast as possible lest they come back up of their own volition before they could work their cure. If you absolutely couldn't stand a raw egg, try one soaked in wine for three days and you'd never crave liquor again. Of course you might still suffer from gout, caused by your previous excesses. Then eat pickled owl as your only meat until the pains vanished. Or try owl broth or jelled liquid. Give a child such broth regularly and it would never become a drunkard.

Feet, Sir Wiliam Jardine.

Snake bite might be cured with a poultice made from the ashes of charred owl's foot. Prevent madness with a similar powder from charred owl eyeballs. And if you wanted some hard-hearted female to tell you the truth about anything, the owl would help you out. Slip in while the lady was asleep and place an owl's heart on her left breast and she would be unable to lie to you. Sometimes the right foot of a Barn-Owl worked just as well as the heart, or you could even use both. Also if a woman wanted to be sure to have a male child, she must never hear an owl calling while she was in labor.

Most of these remedies sound like outright chicanery at worst and at best only a hopeful stab in the very dark realm of coping with human ills. Yet the need for such cures was serious on the part of many an earnest searcher, century after century, and sometimes met with success both in cities and primitive outlands.

The value of dried leaves of the foxglove plant in preventing congestive heart failure and as a diuretic for those suffering from dropsy was known to an old English countrywoman—her name never recorded by the doctors who followed her lead—long before 1775 when patients in Birmingham, England, first profited by its use. Ipecac, the emetic made from dried roots native to Brazil and other lands around the Caribbean, was known to local Indians as "roadside sick-making plant" long before Portuguese explorers took it back to Europe. So-called "witch-doctors" in the Orient and Near East had known how to protect their patients from smallpox with the ooze from sores of cows suffering from a similar but less virulent disease long before vaccination was accepted as standard treatment in Europe and America. None of these success stories happened to involve owls, but it wasn't from lack of trying.

Not all doctors of the earlier centuries thought of owls as a source for medical experiments, however. Pierre Belon, who had earned his medical degree at the University of Paris before deciding that the study of nature for nature's own sake was his calling, described eight owl species in detail without mentioning a single potion in his book published in 1555. But in that same year another physician-turned-naturalist, the eminent Conrad Gesner of Zurich, devoted considerable space in his new book on birds (Book III for his famous *Historia Animalium*) to discussing medical uses of birds. Among some fifteen pages on owls he included numerous dosages best made from night-bird flesh, especially owl brains and liver. A stew of owl brains mingled with whatever tastier food one preferred was suggested as a cure for headaches. Owl brains boiled in sea water till they jelled would form a suppository sure to cure constipation. Owl brains or liver were equally effective in relieving ear ache when blended with olive oil. Or the aromatic ointment known as nard might replace the oil, if desired. Gesner also cited the use of owl eyes in various prescriptions to improve weak vision or prevent drunkenness, as already mentioned here.

Although Gesner sounded confident in the value of his remedies, more reliable cures were still much in demand in Europe. Just fifteen years later Felipe II, king of Spain, sent his own physician—the esteemed Francisco Hernández—to Spain's colony in Mexico for the express purpose of learning how Mexican doctors used plants, animals and minerals in their dosages. Hernández quickly discovered that a fellow Spainard—the Franciscan friar Bernardino de Sahagún who had been in Mexico since 1529—had already compiled such a study as part of his history on "Things of New Spain." Hernández used the friar's description of seven owl species as a basis for his own book, adding more scientific descriptions. But though both men wrote of numerous Aztec remedies neither said much about the medicinal value of owls.

Of these four sixteenth-century owl-watchers, Gesner was the one to give the most attention to medical uses for birds of the owl kind. He also cited more authorities, quoting at least a line or two from almost everyone who had ever written about owl ways, whether naturalist, poet, physician or philosopher. From the Romans he named Virgil, Cicero and Ovid as well as Pliny. From the Greek he cited Aristophanes, Homer and Aesop as well as Aristotle and the physician Galen, and he also quoted the Old Testament Hebrew prophets and Arabic sages.

Sahagún and Hernández were the only ones to describe owl species found only in the New World. After all, they were the only two of the four to know the Americas.

Belon gave us the most detailed descriptions of owl behavior from his own observations. He was also the most impressed with the many likenesses between owls and cats in actions, appearance and yowling voice.

Pierre Belon.

Conrad Gesner.

8

THE CATNESS OF OWLS

PICTURE YOURSELF LOLLING in your easy chair in the half-dusk of an early spring evening, the book you meant to read still unopened on your lap and your cat drowsing contentedly beside you. The scene is set, and you notice how the cat's ears remain alertly upright even though its eyes are closed, its body relaxed as if it is fully asleep. Suddenly those ears twitch sharply, and twitch again in obvious response to some outside noise mere human ears could not catch. The furry body tenses in a magnificent all-muscles-ready leap for its favorite lookout post on the windowsill. Even as it arrives in spectacular four-paws landing your ears get the message, too—the stuttery *woo-oo, wu-wu-wu woo-oo* call of a Western Screech-Owl that comes bounding through the gloom like notes plucked from some ghost-voiced bass viol.

You listen, marveling at the keenness of cat hearing, at the feline ability to keep its senses alert even in sleep. As your eyes follow where cat eyes lead you—to the low-hanging branch of a maple tree beside the red rock wall—you see the stutterer himself, body hunched and motionless, tufted head slightly a-tilt, bright eyes wide open and staring with fixed gaze at a certain hole between the rocks where something just took shelter from owl talons. And you are suddenly aware of how catlike is the owl pose, how closely the feathered body on the maple branch is matched in outline by the furry body on the sill.

There's nothing remarkable about the match, except that you haven't really noticed it before. Both animals are after the same prey. Both are ruled by the same inborn urge to chase any small furry creature that skitters into view—rat, mouse, vole, mole, anything with four legs and fur that runs for a hideyhole. Both know the same inborn command to sit and wait with no betraying sound or movement for whatever went inside to come out again.

When you think about it, there's still further reason for cats and owls to behave like two of a kind. Both hiss in spitfire explosion when angry or annoyed. Both have see-in-the-dark eyes that enable them to hunt when many other predators must call it a day. Both spend much of the daylight hours dozing, and only closer human acquaintance with cats makes our word "cat-naps" more familiar than "owl-naps" in everyday speech. Also, bristly owl face feathers give the same tactile warning as cat whiskers when sense of touch must replace sight.

For another likeness, both hunt reptiles as well as rodents. Both also hunt small birds, and if you regret that choice of prey, then give the songbirds in your yard the best refuge nature can provide—a thick and thorny evergreen hedge where they can take safe shelter when either cats or owls appear on the scene. Firethorn, barberry, catbriar and other such plantings pruned in tight clumps or a hedge are as good as a fortress and both you and your birds will be grateful for its presence.

Meanwhile, glance through the writings of those who discovered the catness of owls long before you. "Cat Owl" has been a common nickname for the Great Horned Owl almost from the very moment European settlers first saw this American species. And "Little Cat Owl" has been an alias for Screech-Owls just as long. The Long-eared Owl has sometimes shared the name, too.

Oddly, the nickname was seldom in common use back in England. And other Europeans who did use it generally meant the tuftless Tawny Owl, not *Bubo* or others with pointed feather tufts to match cat silhouette. Perhaps *Bubo* was too bold a hunter to waste time on copycat waiting at mouse holes, while the Tawny is an avid mouser. At any rate, *kattuggla* is the Tawny's name in Sweden, and in France the label *chathuant*, "hooting cat," gives the Tawny another vote for feline likeness.

In oldtime folktales cats and owls shared the role of companion for witches and other mischief-making spirits. When Shakespeare set the witch scene in *Macbeth,* Act IV, he not only had the hags toss an owl's wing into their brew (*howlet* was his precise term) but had each mention her companion in trouble-making—a cat for one, an owl for another, and for the third a toad. This last doesn't seem to fit until you check the guide books and read that the hoot of a Scops Owl (a European species much like our Screech-Owls in size and coloring) is almost exactly duplicated by the croak of a Midwife Toad—a species in which the male glues the eggs to his hind legs and carries them about till they hatch—so perhaps the owl-like voice won the toad its place.

Alexander Wilson, the Scottish-born American ornithologist who compiled his portraits and descriptions of birds in the first years of the 19th century, regarded both cats and owls as his enemies since both preyed upon the songbirds he loved so dearly. Perhaps the strength of his feeling against them led him to stress their likeness. In describing his first owl entry—Mottled Owl, gray color phase Eastern Screech-Owl—he let himself deliver a diatribe against all owls as creatures the "God of Nature" had punished by making them similar to beasts of prey and preventing them from knowing the full enjoyment of daylight and sunshine. He admitted they were useful, but still insisted Heaven "stamped their countenance with the strong traits of that other murderer, the cat."

Nevertheless, Wilson was scientist enough to keep a live owl in his room to study at close range, and again mentioned its catlike ways, its habit of sitting with half-shut eyes as cats do in full daylight. He wondered at the marvel of its silent flight, and since cats couldn't be blamed for that trick in mouse-hunting, he compared noiseless owl wings to the silence of unnameable "spirits." He described how small birds recognize owls as "evil" and prove it by uniting in shrieking mob attack on any owl caught napping in daytime retreat, "like crowds in the streets of a large city, when a thief or murderer is detected." Among these supposedly virtuous protesters he named the Blue Jay—which he had previously labeled "most bitter enemy to the owl" though still admitting the jay far from guiltless in similar depredation and often equally in need of a hasty getaway from mob attack. However, he never expressed the admiration for owls that he gave the Blue Jay for its cleverness and jaunty elegance. But at least he kept to more objective comments in his entries on other owls.

Some forty years later the philosopher-naturalist of Walden Pond, the not-yet-famous Henry David Thoreau, was also moved to write about the catness of owls. No scorn or condemnation here. And it was not just the likeness of similar silhouettes, for he was watching a round-head Barred Owl that winter day, a bird

> ... *sitting on one of the lower dead limbs of a white pine, close to the trunk, in broad daylight, I standing within a rod of him. He could hear me when I moved and cronched the snow with my feet, but could not plainly see me. When I made most noise he would stretch out his neck, and erect his neck feathers, and*

*open his eyes wide; but their lids soon fell again, and he
began to nod. I too felt a slumberous influence after
watching him half an hour, as he sat thus with his eyes
half open, like a cat, winged brother of the cat. There
was only a narrow slit left between their lids, by which
he preserved a peninsular relation to me; thus, with
half-shut eyes, looking out from the land of dreams,
and endeavoring to realize me, vague object or mote
that interrupted his visions. At length, on some louder
noise or my nearer approach, he would grow uneasy
and sluggishly turn about on his perch, as if impatient
at having his dreams disturbed; and when he launched
himself off and flapped through the pines, spreading
his wings to unexpected breadth, I could not hear the
slightest sound from them. Thus, guided amid the pine
boughs rather by a delicate sense of their neighborhood
than by sight, feeling his twilight way, as it were, with
his sensitive pinions, he found a new perch where he
might in peace await the dawning of his day.*

You read the lines again—if you're an owl-watcher—
first to find that perfect phrase *winged brother of the cat*,
and fix it in memory and then to savor once more the
mood he could create with mere words, letting us share it
all with him as if we had been there, too, that winter day.
And perhaps if we are lucky it will bring back some savory
owl-watching moments of our own that otherwise might
have been forgotten. Like the Barred Owl on another
pine-tree branch one winter day, this time on a South
Carolina sea island, with half-shut eyes and tolerant
acceptance of human intrusion—at least as long as we
stood still in admiring awe.

Cats and owls are also linked in the alphabet picture
books we used to know back in the days when learning
ones letters was the first schoolroom challenge. "C" is for
Cat, "O" is for Owl. Sometimes the owl pictured had the
twin feather tufts of the Great Horned Owl and smaller
Screech-Owls, but almost as often "O" marked the heart-
shaped face of the Barn-Owl.

Boston Public Library.

Any discussion of cats and owls is even more likely to recall a delightful piece of rhymed nonsense from the pen of that remarkable owl-watcher Edward Lear. It's "The Owl and the Pussy-Cat," of course. First published in London in 1871 and reprinted—and joyfully re-read— many times thereafter. For Lear it's the differences between the two that make cat and owl so entrancing a pair, not their likeness. No sitting at a mousehole for them when Edward Lear is telling the story. Off they go on a

107

romantic adventure—and in a boat, of all things, when neither is really a water-lover, although both like fish. But here they eat mince and quince and with a utensil no one ever heard of before Lear decided a runcible spoon was the inevitable choice. Whether he made up that word out of the sounds that marched in his head at the moment or gave a twist to an old printing term— *rounceval,* a curved spoonlike handle on a hand press—is not known. But no question about who were first to use this scooplike spoon with a cutting edge.

If there's no recollection of this odd piece of tableware in your memory of Lear's rhyme, you probably knew only one of the many printings with just the first verse instead of all three. You will see this short-change version often, especially in books for young children—perhaps to avoid questions about taking a trip together before marriage instead of afterward as propriety requires—or used to. But here only the entire story will do.

> The Owl and the Pussy-Cat went to sea
> In a beautiful pea-green boat.
> They took some honey and plenty of money
> Wrapped up in a five-pound note.
> The Owl looked up to the stars above,
> And sang to a small guitar,
> "Oh lovely Pussy! O Pussy my love!
> What a beautiful Pussy you are—
> You are;
> What a beautiful Pussy you are!"
>
> Pussy said to the Owl, "You elegant fowl,
> How charmingly sweet you sing!
> Oh, let us be married—too long we have tarried—
> But what shall we do for a ring?"
> They sailed away for a year and a day,
> To the land where the bong tree grows;
> And there, in a wood, a Piggy-wig stood—
> With a ring at the end of his nose,
> His nose;
> With a ring at the end of his nose.

"Dear Pig, are you willing to sell for one shilling
    "Your ring?" Said the Piggy, "I will."
So they took it away and were married next day
    By the Turkey who lives on the hill.
They dined upon mince and slices of quince,
    Which they ate with a runcible spoon;
And hand in hand, on the edge of the sand,
    They danced by the light of the moon—
        The moon;
    They danced by the light of the moon.

9

OWLS ARE COLLECTIBLE

No one seems to know when or where collecting articles with owl motif became a fad for North Americans. But sometime in the 1950s anyone involved with antiques, art galleries, museums, jewelry stores, gift shops, variety stores and souvenir stands began to realize people *liked* owls—and were ready to buy almost anything in owl shape or with owl design. By the 1960s, collecting owliana was no longer a fad but a full-fledged hobby.

Perhaps this friendly feeling for owls had to wait until few people were seeing owls in the wild, never caught them snatching a robin from the lawn or a frightened bunny from a grass clump. Also, many artists with owls to sell took care to soften their hunter's glare to friendly gaze, masked the predator with scholar's cap and gown and spectacles, even added an air of cartoon cuteness. In addition, the changing attitude toward all predators was a factor, as more people accepted each species as nature made it, understanding the killing is for survival, not bloodlust or glory.

For most collectors, the fun is in having trophies to display so others can see and admire. But for those with little room and less time and energy for keeping displays in order, the happiest collecting can be of memories— sometimes of owls seen in the wild or in zoos, but also museums specimens, pictures in books and art galleries and especially prehistoric rock carvings.

The oldest portrayal of owls now known dates back some 17,000 years or more to southern France at the end of the Ice Age when lingering glacial snow and ice gave the craggy hills an almost Arctic climate.

People lived in caves, keeping those easiest of entry for family rooms or gathering places, and reserving the deeper inner chambers for tribal elders or others earning special privileges. Many of the chambers had walls covered with drawings cut with a sharp-edged stone through the darkened outer surface to the paler rock beneath. Sometimes colors were added, sometimes not.

On this day when we imagine ourselves there among the cavedwellers, someone was holding just such a marking stone in his hand. Perhaps he was a boy who only moments before had been acknowledged a man in tribal rite. Now he was privileged to explore as he chose, alone, and he left the ceremonial room to follow a narrow corridor's twisting and turning, lifting his torch higher from time to time to see whatever its flickering light might reveal. Abruptly the corridor opened into a wider gallery and there on the dark wall at his left was a space a full arm's length, smooth and untouched by outcrop or crevice. The stone in his hand moved almost of itself as he began to fill that smooth dark space with the picture that had all at once leaped into his mind, demanding to take its ordained place on that untouched wall.

The stone cut deep, marking a round head with one line, close-held wing with another. Then a line or two more and he had the likeness of a bird he knew well, the big white-feathered owl with the gleaming yellow eyes. A few lines more made the nest in its fringe of grasses.... then another owl on the nest's far side ... and then a few last lines for the just-hatched chick in the nest between the parents and he was finished. He stood back to look at it, smiling, then snatched up his torch while it could still light his way and hurried back to the others.

Why did he draw these Snowy Owls and not some other bird or beast? Why a mated pair and chick instead of a fierce-eyed adult plunging to capture unwarned prey? Was he—perhaps—trying to express his acceptance of just-gained adulthood, his understanding that taking a mate, defending her and their home from enemies, hunting to feed her and their young were the requirements of the role he must now fill?

Or was he an old man, nearing his last days, taking this way to sum up what for him had been most meaningful in life's pattern?

Or—whether old or young—did he have no reason at all except that owls were birds he knew well and admired and here he stood with a good cutting stone in hand and an untouched wall before him?

Centre d'Etudes Prehistorique, France.

Whatever the questions, they will never be answered. But the owls are still there on the cave wall, first put on history's written record in 1918 but not thoroughly studied for another forty years. Three brothers were first to find the drawing and so "Three Brothers"—*Trois Frères*—is the cave's name and the corridor where the picture was drawn is *Gálerie des Chouettes. Chouette*—literally "little cabbage"—was not in early use, but applied when watchers finally realized owls might be put in two groups: those with heads round like cabbages and those with tufts. *Chouette* has also been considered a good imitation of a typical owl hiss or sneezy cough. Either way, the French use it now for all tuftless owls, with each such species further identified by an added word of description. For the Snowy the full name is *Chouette Harfang*, Round-head Hare-catcher.

There are owl figures carved on rocks in North America, too. They may not be so old as the pair in the *Gálerie des Chouettes* but they are equally fascinating and much easier to visit. Some of them fairly easy to find are on the rocks beside Rochester Creek, a small stream draining into the Muddy River about fifty miles south of Price, Utah. These owls—like the other animals and people pictured here—are stylized, but they are quickly identified by their typically large eyes, head tufts and widespread wings. One of them, positioned just above a rainbow-shaped arch of lines, has its tufts set close together toward the center of the head, and so may be intended as a Long-eared Owl instead of the Great Horned, whose tufts are farther apart. The human pictured beside it is much smaller than the bird, suggesting the owl was of importance in tribal ritual or as a personal deity for the artist and perhaps esteemed for its magic powers.

Malcolm and Louise Loring.

Somewhat similar stylized owls were once easily seen among the rock carvings along the north bank of the Columbia River. Other figures were there, too—birds, animals, people, geometric designs. But owls were a specialty in the area now outlining the river banks of Skamania and Klickitat Counties in the State of Washington, just across the river from the city of The Dalles, Oregon. Most of them were at the eastern edge of Klickitat County on the rugged basalt cliffs that hemmed in a narrow ravine known as Petroglyph Canyon. The canyon is still there, but no one will ever walk through it again, for it was engulfed by the flooding waters that swept over much of this area with the completion of The Dalles Dam by U.S. Army Engineers in 1959.

Luckily, the dam took so long to build that archaeologists and historians could save some Indian artifacts and rock art. Amateurs and professionals alike went all out to copy, photograph and take rubbed transfers of the petroglyphs, scrounging and scrambling among the rocks.

Among the photographers were Malcolm Loring of the U.S. Forest Service and his wife Louise, whose photograph is shown here. The Army Engineers also managed to break off a few basalt slabs with the drawings intact, now on display in the outdoor visitor's area of the Dam Project Offices in The Dalles at the city's eastern limits.

No date has been established for the Petroglyph Canyon owl carvings. Not even the century is known. There is little way to date rock art except by artifacts found near it. Most of the artifacts found so far have been from the early nineteenth century when Meriwether Lewis and William Clark first came this way and the Indians they talked with would not identify the canyon artists except as "Old Ones," disclaiming all relationship. But recently artifacts discovered only a few miles to northward have been dated as at least 11,000 years old.

Whoever the artists were, they knew one owl from another and identified the Great Horned Owl by always showing prominent feather tufts, large eyes and wide, wide wings. The drawings are so similar you might think them done by the same artist, or at least by several artists all following a design prescribed by tribal authorities. They are also stylized, almost as stylized as letters of the alphabet, and it is possible that tribal custom dictated their design as strictly as our dictionaries dictate the spelling of o-w-l.

Whether the owl was feared or revered—or both—we do not know. Nor can we give it the name the artist used, for the language of the tribe and its own name are lost. Instead of using the name of a contemporary tribe or family, we label them Petroglyph Canyon owls, thankful we know even this little. Did the owl figures mark a place where ceremonies were held asking the owl to use its magic in the artist's favor? Did they show a crevice where owls had nested or where some tribal Wise One had seen an owl in a dream or in reality? We can say only that owls would scarcely have been portrayed so often if there had been no bond of any kind between the birds and the artists.

The glyph wall carvings on the Washington side of the Columbia are not the only owl figures to be rescued in these years. The Oregon Archaeological Society was especially active on both sides of the river, hurrying to get digging rights from private landowners before flooding waters could come rushing in to cover all. Fern and Frank Sauke were digging on the Washington side that March day in 1958 when—after turning up various fragments and small objects including a well-used smoker's pipe with beaver-tail shape— they found an owl-faced figure carved from columnar basalt and still bearing traces of the red ochre paint that often decorated the more ornate figures. Its height—nearly two feet—match the size of a living Great Horned Owl and the ear tufts, though worn, add further identification and the Saukes promptly dubbed it *Bubo*, relying on Latin since no Indian name is known.

On the Oregon side other Society members were finding owl trophies among the tons of rubble they sifted with backbreaking work. Occasionally these fragments could be pieced together to form whalebone clubs or grinding stones and mortars. Each piece was a trophy to be studied, but the most exciting find—real treasure trove—came when John Krussow began digging into an odd-looking rock pile that nature had unearthed in a mammoth rock slide. The pieces he uncovered were not only in fragments. They were also blackened by ancient fires. But they had obviously been placed there in layers, and at different times.

A cremation pit, Krussow deduced, thinking such charred and scattered fragments would tell little of who had done the burying or who had been buried. But then his fingers touched something of solid shape and he worked it loose, held it up with a look of awed wonder and delight. Somehow a miniature mortar bowl in owl form had escaped damage from both rocks and fire—except for a small sooty smudge—and there it was, whole, unblemished, almost as the artist himself would last have seen it when he placed it with the other burial offerings beside the body.

John Krussow

This artist had been no copier of stylized glyphs. He—or perhaps she—had worked with a sure hand guided by eyes that knew well the bird to emerge from the pale-hued, fine-grained stone. A round face topped by earlike lobes to represent the feather tufts, a sharply down-curved beak, eyes large and round, spread wings and tail marked for feathering. Beyond all doubt it is an owl, and probably a Great Horned Owl.

This miniature is just 4¾ inches high, 4½ inches long, with arched wings 3½ inches across. The hollow scooped from its body to make the mortar bowl is 2 inches across and 1 inch deep—too small for actual use in grinding grain, although possibly large enough for preparing a single dose of medicine. The ritual gifts offered in crema-tion ceremonies and other burial rites were often minia-tures, symbolic of all the good things that would be

117

waiting in the future world envisioned by tribal tradition. The beauty of the workmanship tells of the artist's skill and perhaps of the esteem granted the deceased. Either the artist or the one so honored could have been a woman, for legends about the Old Ones of Columbia River country say women often served as chieftains and in other roles reserved more often for men. As to this artist's sex or rank we can only guess. And there is only a guess for the century in which the owl mortar was placed in the pit, since the rock slide destroyed all evidence of which artifact had originally been in which layer or even whether the layers were still in their original sequence. An estimate of between 600 and 1,200 years ago has been given for the cremation date. But the date does not really matter for collectors of owl memories. The picture and the story are enough.

For those who want more glimpses of the past, an owl hunt through museums can yield innumerable artifacts. What do you want to see most? Paintings, crystal, pottery, metalwork, stamps, coins, wood, stone or handcraft of all kinds, any kind? Among the oldest owl artifacts you will find on museum display are bronze vessels from ancient China, perhaps dating to 1500, 1600 or more years B.C. Examples of these can be found in the Minneapolis Institute of Arts, Yale University Art Gallery, Art Institute of Chicago or the Fogg Art Museum in Cambridge, Massachusetts.

Tomb paintings and sculpture from Egypt are equally old. In the Money Museum of the Chase Manhattan Bank and in the museum of the American Numismatic Society—both in New York—are actual Athenian owl coins. They're also on display in museums in Athens, Berlin, Bologna, Paris, London and Oxford. Coins offered for sale recently were priced from $180 to $2,750 depending on condition and rarity of that particular issue and on whether the coin was all silver or silver plate on bronze. In New York also the American Indian Heye Foundation has owl art among its displays and so does the American Museum of Natural History. In fact, any natural history museum or historical museum of any kind anywhere might well have work with owl motif among its collections, perhaps items that have not yet had the attention owl collectors will give them. For more modern work, consider original owl paintings by Audubon and Wilson and other 19th century artists or even the less expensive prints from their published books. Prints from Audubon's smaller American edition of the 1840s are more often available and far less costly than those of his "Elephant Folio."

Shops catering to collectors of coins or stamps or fine porcelains may have displays you'll enjoy, too, whether or not you're ready to buy. And don't forget the local craft fairs. Prices may be a lot more reasonable than at the shops and the work excellent, as anyone with a true eye for owls will learn at once. Often you'll find advertisements for owl figures in nature magazines, or magazines specializing in home decor. Some of these—especially porcelains by Boehm, Cybis and other famous houses—may be priced in the thousands of dollars, especially for limited editions. Others, such as those by Franklin Mint, Lalique, Lenox, or Maruri are priced in the hundreds. Some double, triple or quadruple in value in a few years. Some don't. But that's a matter for investors to consider, not for collectors—and especially not for collectors of memories.

Stamps with owl motif may be the least expensive item to collect and take up the least room. However, costs can go up a bit—and fun as well—if you plan to visit the country in which each stamp was issued and look for the pictured owl right there in its native haunts. Stamps featuring the Eagle Owl, for instance, could take you to Afghanistan, Finland, France, Germany, Hungary, Poland, Romania, Sweden, Yugoslavia and probably several other places you'd like to see. The 1939 French stamp—value 65 centimes—bears the label *Grand Duc* to remind you of how the tufted owls achieved ducal rank.

Postage stamps from U.S.A., Monaco, France, and Hungary.

Stamps picturing the *Petit Duc* (alias Scops Owl) will add Israel, Korea and Poland to your itinerary. The Barn-Owl will escort you to Monaco. A 1962 stamp not only pictures the owl but adds a plug for the protection of all useful birds—a category for which the rat-catching Barn-Owl is well qualified but seldom receives.

If settling down in your easy chair with a good owl book sounds more inviting than travel, you have plenty to choose from. Whatever other favorites you may have, don't miss the most incredible owl story ever told—the one guaranteed to bring raised eyebrows every time you re-tell it.

Who first told this strangest of all owl stories is not known. But it was first published in the year 1679 in Paris as one of the famous fables of Jean de La Fontaine. And he maintained firmly that it had been told to him by one who had seen it happen and could swear it was true. Furthermore, it was also verified as true some sixty years later by a French Jesuit priest, Pierre François Xavier de Charlevoix, who said he had actually seen such wonders when traveling in Canada—*Nouvelle France,* as the French then called it. Charlevoix's history of his travels was translated to English in 1866, spreading the story still further. La Fontaine's version was already in rhymed translation by the American versifier Elizur Wright, whose fables were in print in Boston in 1841. Wright's idea of attesting to the authenticity of the tale was to say it was as undisputable as the interest calculated in your bank book. Like La Fontaine, Wright also declared the story proved beyond doubt that owls can reason as logically as any scholar.

As the story goes, an owl once made its home in a fallen pine tree in which the wear of time and weather had provided cavities for both roosting and storage of any mice he could capture beyond daily need. Such food supplies were essential in winter when snow and ice often made hunting next to impossible, and the owl started to fill his storage holes in good time. To keep the mice alive for tastier dining later, he brought them food each day and to keep them from escaping he carefully bit off their feet. What reasoning! Wright assured his readers, adding:

> *Now find me, in your human schools,*
> *A better use for logic's tools!*
> *Upon your faith, what different art of thought*
> *Has Aristotle or his followers taught?*

Wright must have known his logical Bostonian readers would challenge his claim, for he added a footnote putting all the responsibility on La Fontaine. And since the illustrator showed the owl in tidy white apron and cap, New Englanders could only shrug it off as one more tale a little too tall for anything but admiration that truth could be stretched so far.

Yet if you sift through the story for whatever kernels of truth may lurk beneath the fantasy, some facts are hiding there. Owls do often collect more prey than they can eat at the moment, especially when there are owlets to feed. Birdwatchers who check on nests often report finding the bodies of two or three rats, mice, rabbits, squirrels—even fish—carefully stacked at the side of the nest ready for later use. Of course these lay-aways are dead before they are brought home. At least they are supposed to be. But anyone who has seen a mouse go limp in a cat's jaws then suddenly come to life the moment the jaws relax their grip, might concede that a mouse could fool an owl, also. Maybe not for long, but possibly—just possibly—long enough.

Another kernel adds a shadow of credence even to the bitten feet. Owls have long since learned to raid traps set out by humans, and if the victim is held fast by only its front feet, one quick bite and then another and the owl has dinner in its own talons and off it goes. A traveler fresh from European city life could see the bitten feet and credit the owl with remarkable trickery if not logic. An even more fantastic tale than La Fontaine's could have been written by Alexander Wetmore if he hadn't been an expert on owl behavior, for in Wyoming one summer he found the nest of a Long-eared Owl surrounded by the traps Wetmore himself had put out to take a small-mammal census for the Smithsonian. Obviously the owls had found it easier to fly home with trap and contents, eat the captives as needed and let the emptied traps lie where they fell. Wetmore told his story in a book to be published by National Geographic, not as fable, and he gave the owls no more credit than was due.

Neither La Fontaine nor Charlevoix identified the owl hero of their stories. But if Canada is the setting and the roosting place a fallen pine tree, the Northern Hawk-Owl seems the likeliest candidate, although the Great Horned Owl has also nested in stumps instead of the usual lofty aerie. But who demands the accuracy of banker's arithmetic for a tale that has no need for truth to make it worth reading?

Among the most memorable owl figures in any collection are the kachina owl dolls made by Hopi Indians of Arizona. Although they are called "dolls" because of their size, they were never meant as toys. For the Hopis, kachinas are the sacred spirits of animals who had befriended tribal ancestors long, long ago when the world was new and both animals and humans shared each other's lives.

Even when the world changed and animals and humans lived apart, Hopis believed their old companions might return as invisible spirits to offer guidance. To represent their presence certain worthy men were chosen to impersonate these spirits for tribal ceremonies by wearing helmet masks and matching animal costumes so their own individuality would not intrude on the kachina identity. As part of the ceremony, the story of how the animal ancestor had befriended Hopi ancestors would be told again, lest it be forgotten. From time to time, children now old enough to understand the stories were invited to take part in some game or contest. Winners would receive a kachina doll as prize, not to play with but as a symbol of the tribal tradition that was now theirs to cherish and remember.

Three kinds of owls are among the kachinas. Most important, most respected is Monwu the Great Horned Owl. The other two--Hotsko and Salak—also wear feather-tufted masks but are smaller and may represent a Screech-Owl and the Flammulated Owl. As the story-tellers explain, the owls helped Hopi ancestors by sharing their secret of how silence can be the best way to bring both success for the hunter and safety for the hunted.

Children needed to learn the secret of safety for the hunted first. In olden days, raiding enemies might descend at any time upon a Hopi village, and as the men rushed out to fight, the women and children would hurry to hide among the rocks of a nearby canyon. There even the youngest child must learn to keep quiet, make no move-ment, make no sound that might betray their presence when the enemy raiders passed by. At the festival the kachinas would play a game chosen to help make the lesson one no child would forget.

U.S. Bureau of Ethnology.

Usually only men wore kachina costumes, but for the game teaching the owls' secret of silence, a woman and two or three children were also in owl costume. First Owl Woman led the children to the center of the ring formed by watching villagers. And at that very moment the owl kachinas— somewhere in hiding—would begin a hooting chorus.

The children look up at Owl Woman, knowing her fright is only pretense, knowing what she will say and what they must do, but still trembling as she gives them a shove, calling her warning:

"Owls are coming! Owls are coming!
Quick, now! Quiet, now! Run and hide!
Quick, before big owl eyes see you!
Quiet, lest sharp owl ears hear you!
Owls are coming! Owls! Owls! Owls!"

And here they come, prancing, dancing with rhythmic step and stomp. Shaking their gourd rattles, pretending to search here and there, behind this, under that, but making sure they do not see the children and shouting out new threats:

"If we hear you, we can find you.
If we find you, we will eat you,
Eat you up all in one bite.
Just one bite and you'll be gone"

And Owl Woman calls encouragement and reminder with:

"Quiet, my children, do not cry.
Be quiet and owls will pass you by."

Of course they are quiet. And the owls pantomime their disgust at finding nothing to eat and beckon each other to look elsewhere, pointing toward the goats grazing some-where just beyond, just out of sight. And sounds of bleating goats and hooting owls come drifting back, getting fainter and fainter until at last Owl Woman calls the children to come out of hiding, praising them for keeping so quiet even when a prancing owl almost stepped on them. And all the Hopis gather round to praise them, too, keeping the talk going until those who imper-sonated the owls have time to reappear as themselves and present each of the children with an owl kachina along

125

with a reminder to watch owls for themselves and see how well the night birds remember the secret of silence.

"Watch and learn!" some elder is almost sure to say. "Watching is the beginning of wisdom."

MONWÛ

U.S. Bureau of Ethnology.

10
HOW AND WHERE
TO WATCH OWLS

THE BEST OWL WATCHING you'll ever have may happen without any planning, simply a matter of luck. For one beginning birdwatcher in Portland, Oregon, luck arrived on a winter morning when she looked out her kitchen window and saw a big white bird perched on her garage roof.

"Funny-looking gull," she thought, but then the "gull" turned its big round head to stare at her with great yellow eyes set side by side in a rounded face and she gasped amazed contradiction.

"No! A Snowy Owl! A Snowy! It has to be!"

And of course it was. She'd studied owl pictures in her bird book too many times to miss, even if she'd never seen a Snowy before.

So, the first good rule for owl watchers is to know how to identify whatever owls you may see, wherever you happen to see them, even if they show up in unlikely places. Learn how to tell owls from other birds, then learn how to tell one owl from another.

Little Horn Owle,
Francis Willughby.

The owl silhouette is unique, not like any other bird's, so keep looking at every bird you see—in the wild or zoos or even museum specimens and pictures—until you can recognize the owl shape at a glance. First, owls have bigger and rounder heads—in proportion to body size— than other birds. When perched on a branch they sit erect but still with a dumpy, no-neck shape that makes a typical owl ID clue. When hiding or napping they seem to shrink inside their feathers and look much smaller than usual. So when they suddenly take a threatening pose with all feathers ruffled or soar off skyward, they may surprise you with their bulk—and especially with the width of their wings, for most owls have far wider wingspan than other birds of the same body size.

Owls often—but not always—have much shorter tails than other birds of similar length. And when you see them full face you have the easiest clue of all—those two owl eyes side by side in a rounded face. The short curved beak, so close to the face, is an added clue you probably won't need, but it's there to complete your ID checklist just the same.

Nineteen species of owls nest north of Mexico and each

one will be described in the following pages. Each one has certain features, or a combination of features, no other species possesses. Learning these ID clue marks for all nineteen species may take a while, so begin with one or two you're most likely to see or rate highest on your wish-list. The same system holds good for all, and each one you add will be easier. Just four clues will identify any owl from all the others, and the first clue is size, body-length from head to tail. No need to know the precise measurement in inches given in the bird books. As you've probably noticed, females are usually larger than males and even individuals of the same sex and species may vary by several inches, making precise comparison of a single bird impossible. Instead, think of the median length as compared to the length of your arm—or whatever span best matches the lengths of the five size groups for owls. These groups are:

Super-large	22-30 inches
Large	16-20 inches
Medium	14-18 inches
Small	8-12 inches
Very Small	5-7 inches

If your arm doesn't seem to fit, you may find it easier to judge sizes by comparison to some familiar birds. Red-tailed Hawk, Herring Gull or Raven for the Supers. Common Crow for the Large, Robins for Medium, Starling or Redwinged Blackbird for Small and House Sparrow for the Very Small. You can learn to judge these lengths at a glance—with a little practice—always remembering to match for length only, not for the bulk of the body or the ratio of length between tail and body.

Once you're fairly accurate with size judgment, you'll find the other three clues can be seen in a glance. For the second clue, note whether the head is tufted or rounded. For the third, check iris color—either yellow-to-orange or dark (brown or smokey black but still plainly dark as opposed to the bright yellow-orange). For the fourth, notice the color of body plumage: brown, gray, rufous, buff-and-white, speckled white. Just five basic colors for owls, and only occasionally will two species be so much alike you also need to notice further markings.

All four clues may be needed for identification or sometimes only one or two, but size always has to be judged first. For instance, both Snowy and Barn-Owls are white on face, belly and wing linings as they fly toward you, but the Snowy is Super-large, almost twice the length of the Medium Barn-Owl. Judge size first and you can't miss. Also both the Great Horned Owl and the Long-eared are brown, yellow-eyed and tufted, but the size difference is obvious. The following "Quick ID Chart" will be a handy reference as you begin learning species differences.

QUICK ID CHART

SUPER LARGE
(3 species: Great Horned Owl, Great Gray Owl, Snowy Owl)
Tufted—Great Horned Owl
Round-headed—Great Gray Owl, Snowy Owl
Speckled-white—Snowy Owl

LARGE
(2 species: Barred Owl, Spotted Owl)
Round-headed—Barred Owl, Spotted Owl
Dark-eyed—Barred Owl, Spotted Owl
Brown—Barred Owl, Spotted Owl
Vertical belly markings—Barred Owl
Horizontal belly markings—Spotted Owl

MEDIUM
(4 species: Common Barn-Owl, Hawk-Owl,
Long-eared Owl, Short-eared Owl)
Tufted—Long-eared Owl, Short-eared Owl
Dark eyes—Common Barn-Owl
Horizontal black belly Markings—Hawk-Owl

SMALL

(4 species: Boreal Owl, Burrowing Owl,
Western and Eastern Screech-Owls)
Tufted—Western and Eastern Screech-Owl
Face distinctly outlined in black—Boreal Owl
Long, unfeathered legs—Burrowing Owl

VERY SMALL

(6 species: Whiskered Owl, Saw-whet Owl, Northern Pygmy-
Owl, Ferruginous Pygmy-Owl, Flammulated Owl, Elf Owl)
Prominent tufts—Whiskered Owl
Dark eyes—Flammulated Owl
Rufous with *short* tail, solid-colored back—Saw-whet Owl
Rufous, *long* tail, solid-colored back—Ferruginous Pygmy-Owl
Rufous, *long* tail, speckled back—Northern Pygmy-Owl
Sandy brown—Elf Owl

Further details of coloring, range and habitat to help
you with identifying similar species are given on following pages, but the clues on the chart will get you started
on the right track.

Of course owling experts can also offer helpful advice
on how and when and where to go on an owling
adventure. An article in *American Birds,* for instance,
suggests you be sure to match typical habitat when you're
looking for a particular species. If you're looking for a
Short-eared Owl, try flatlands near airports or marshy
prairies; for Great Horned Owls you'll want the woods. Of
course either one can turn up almost anywhere, but you're
more likely to find them in the habitat they prefer.

James Davis, Educational Director of the Portland
Audubon Society, suggests you'll usually see more owls—
even the strictly nocturnal species—if you go when there is
enough light for your eyes—at dusk or dawn instead of
after full dark, or on cloudy days or even at midnight if
there's a full moon. A good flashlight is a must for safety's
sake, but it usually frightens the owls away before you
catch more than a glance, so use it only for emergencies as

long as the light holds. It's possible to avoid alarming the owls if you cover the lens of your flashlight with red plastic or thin red silk, since owls are red-blind at night. Whether the red filter does enough good to be worthwhile is a matter of opinion, however. Davis also suggests you prepare your eyes for adjustment to dim light by sitting in a darkened room for 10 or 15 minutes before you start on your owl walk.

George Laycock, field editor for *Audubon Magazine,* warns you to carry insect repellent if you're owling in bug-biting season. Even if you can ignore the itching, trying to swat mosquitoes and watch owls at the same time isn't too successful.

Almost all experts agree you should dress for comfort and for the weather. Wear waterproof boots and garments if they're needed and especially have sturdy comfortable shoes. Almost all experts also agree it's best to scout the area the day before you plan an owl prowl—and go by daylight when you can spot tricky places—mudholes, quicksand, rock slides or whatever else might lead to misstep and possible injury.

Plan-ahead scouting will also enable you to spot where owls are most likely to appear later. Notice any tree cavities of rock crevices that might serve as nest or roost. A hard rap below the hole may bring an owl to the opening and verify its presence. Usually one special roost—often the top of a storm-damaged tree—is used when eating any large prey the owl can't swallow on the wing. Owls gulp down their prey whole, or in large chunks, for as Audubon discovered on dissecting a Snowy, the stomach is thin-walled and capable of great extension. Later they regurgitate undigestible bones, fur and feathers, now all rolled together in a tidy pellet by strong owl stomach muscles. One pellet per day per owl. After a roosting tree has been used for feasting for awhile the ground below is well covered with pellets, and if you make note of its location you can return after dusk with a good chance of catching the owl at its dinner. If you're curious as to what it has been eating, take a few pellets home, let them soak in water overnight and by morning they'll open easily and reveal a crushed mouse skull or bits of fur or feathers or insect casing you may recognize. Almost any time you see a precise list of an owl's menu it has been compiled from pellet checks, though stomach contents may have been examined also.

Most experts agree your first night of owling should be with a group under a leader who knows both the owls and the terrain to be covered. If you don't happen to have such an expert among your friends, check with your local Audubon Society or natural history museum or professional birding tours and find a group you can join. Even after you acquire some expertise of your own—as you will if you keep watching—you'll probably be safer with a companion and happier in sharing whatever befalls. Sooner or later you'll probably want to get a close look at eggs or owlets, but that can be dangerous both for you and the babies. You may keep the owlets from being fed or warmed properly. Some owl parents count anyone coming near the nest as an enemy to be routed with beak and claw—and owl beaks and claws are not gentle. If an owl decides to attack it usually goes for the head, so never go near a nest without hard-hat protection. Above all do NOT wear a fur cap. To owl eyes, especially if you're crouched down in the bushes or plastered against a tree trunk, that fuzzy cap will look like a furry animal and you're likely to have some bloody slashes to remind you of their mistake. Cover your head also if you have a curlytop hairdo that could be mistaken for fur by wary owl eyes. The author's friend, Carolyn, came close to learning the meaning of that old southern phrase "snatched bald-headed" when a Great Horned Owl caught a glimpse of only her head—caught in a patch of lamplight as she leaned over to add a few sticks of kindling to the pile on the porch of her summer cabin—and mistook it for a rabbit or some other fuzzy edible. Down the owl came, talons outstretched, suddenly realised its error and did a backward sommersault leaving only a whoosh of air to mark her narrow escape.

Besides deciding whether or not to look into occupied owl nests, you will probably also have to come to terms with the question of using tape recordings of owl calls to lure owls into the light where you can get a better look. Both of these are difficult decisions and you may consider the owls' well-being more important than satisfying your curiosity. When portable tapes first became available a few years ago, most owlers hailed them as a bonanza to which they were entitled beyond question. Now that owlers have seen how the tapes affect owls, you may not be so sure of your rights.

Although all owls of a given species may sound alike to you, to other owls each is unique. Furthermore, they don't hoot or hiss or click beaks just to hear themselves. They are communicating with other owls, sometimes reassuring a mate, sometimes warning a rival coming too close to established boundary line, sometimes offering courtship invitation. When you play a warning call, for instance, to an owl right in the middle of its own territory, you're causing confusion that may force the owl to move its nest elsewhere. Any of the other calls may result in mischief the owls can't cope with, too. Remember, the damage you do with your tapes is a matter of special concern if a rare species is involved.

In Texas a few years ago the only known nest of Ferruginous Pygmy-Owls in the state got considerable publicity and watchers came pouring in. Most of them had tapes of these owl calls in hand, and played them constantly. The Pygmy pair were kept in a state of tension that didn't bode well for calm nest-tending and successful hatching. A check proved that most of the tapes had been made in Mexico and weren't really a good match for the calls of the Texas birds—double reason for confusion. A pleading notice in *American Birds* asked for cooperation lest the beleaguered pair abandon the one-and-only Texas nest site.

"This pair of owls is taped out," the message read. "Their typical response to a tape is to seek deep cover for long periods of time. Even when the owl calls on its own it is usually a quiet, mellow call. . . . Please leave your owl tape in the car. The birds can be located and observed well by a careful birder."

Whatever you do about owling tactics, remember that owls—like all birds—are found most often where you do the most looking for them. And in spite of the joy in finding a Snowy Owl on your garage roof, the best places to do the most looking are in the kinds of wildland haunts the owls themselves have chosen time and again. Nineteen different owl species are at home here in the North American wilds, each with its own pattern of habits and habitat for you to discover. All nineteen cannot be seen in any single area, but every state—except Hawaii—and every Canadian province and territory has at least three owl species you can watch not too far away from your usual birdwalk trails. If you want to venture a little farther, a recent Christmas Bird Count for the National Audubon Society showed that California owlers saw the most different species—twelve—while British Columbia was second with ten and Oregon and Ontario tied for third place with nine species each. Ten other states from Massachusetts to Ohio to Texas found eight species. Ten more from Maine to Minnesota to Arizona had seven species. Any other year, any other season, the count might vary. But the owls are there. All you need is the luck of being in the right place at the right time.

RANGE MAPS
by Virginia C. Holmgren

Great Horned Owl

Great Gray Owl

Short-eared Owl

Burrowing Owl

Common Barn Owl

Western Screech-Owl

Northern Saw-whet Owl

Northern Pygmy-Owl

Snowy Owl

Barred Owl

Spotted Owl

Long-eared Owl

Northern Hawk Owl

Boreal Owl

Eastern Screech-Owl

Whiskered Screech-Owl

Flamulated Owl

Ferruginous Pygmy-Owl

Elf Owl

137

11
NORTH AMERICAN OWLS

THE NINETEEN SPECIES of owls nesting north of
Mexico are listed here by size as in the "Quick ID Chart"
(page 130) in the preceding chapter. In most other bird
books you'll find them listed by family and genus as is
customary for scientific classifying. You can quickly find
any of these species in such books since the scientific label
is given here beside the American name as listed in official
publications of the American Ornithologists' Union.

Three of Super Size

GREAT HORNED OWL, *Bubo virginianus*
   The "Great Horned" is the most wide-ranging of all
American owls, at home throughout the hemisphere,
seldom missing on any state's Christmas Bird Count. It is
also familiar even to non-owlers as the model for cartoons,
greeting cards and numerous advertisements urging us to
be "wise as an owl."

Great Horned Owl, Alexander Wilson.

Because it looks so much like the Old World Eagle Owl, *Bubo bubo,* it was not published as a unique species until the German-born naturalist Johann Gmelin did so in 1788. However, it had already been described in several American travel diaries including *A Voyage to Carolina* by John Lawson published in London in 1709. To him it was "as big as a middling Goose and has a prodigious Head. They make a fearful Hollowing in the Night-time, like a Man, whereby they often make Strangers lose their way."

● FOLK NAMES: King Owl, Eagle Owl, Big Cat Owl, Winged Tiger, Big-eared Owl, Hoot Owl.

● OTHER NAMES: In French-Canada it is *Le Grand Duc* and in Spanish America it is *Buho Real*—both names borrowed from the Eagle Owl. It is also known by many Indian names including Mexican *tecolote* which imitates the typical call as "tay-co-lo-tay," *tuco* in Peru, *tucuquerre* in Chile.

● ID CLUES: Size—length 18-25 inches; wingspan 49-62 inches. Tufts—prominent, usually slanted outward. Eyes—large and bright yellow. Coloring—mottled brown plumage, white bib under chin. Around Hudson's Bay individuals are usually pale gray (camouflage against snow) and could be mistaken for Great Gray if you forget to note the tufts.

• HABITAT: woodlands, brushy hillsides, cliffs, even well-forested parklands, abandoned orchards. Uses nests of hawks, ravens, etc. or made-to-order imitations you provide or rock crevices.

Great Gray Owl, John James Audubon.

GREAT GRAY OWL, *Strix nebulosa*

A thick-all-over coat of smoky-gray plumage suggested Latin *nebulosa*—"smoke-colored," "mist-colored"—to naturalist Johann Forster when he published the scientific label in London in 1772. At the time, Greco-Latin *strix*—"night hag," "owl"—was the only genus used by most owl classifiers. It is now limited to species with unusually large heads and well-marked facial discs and the Great Gray qualifies on both counts. Thickness of its plumage adds a bulky look, the especially wide and well-outlined facial discs make the head seem even larger and an unusually long tail (for an owl) adds to body length making this species seem the largest of the Supers at casual glance, and measurements usually agree.

As a resident of the Far North this species seldom sees many people and is therefore generally unsuspicious of human misbehavior and shows a trust most people label sheer stupidity. Rocky Mountain heights provide much the same climate as its more northern haunts, and some individuals have followed the mountains southward to make California's Yosemite area a year-round home where they are welcomed with affection. Recently there have been fewer in the park and a special committee has been organized to learn the reasons for owl decline and to suggest remedies.

In the last few years more and more Great Grays are venturing into New England—and even farther south— for the winter. Birdwatchers there are delighted to see them but curious about the reasons. "Guess they tried it, liked it and came again," one observer decided. And as unscientific as that sounds, it could be right.

● FOLK NAMES: Cinerous Owl, Gray Ghost, Spectral Owl, Spruce Owl.

● OTHER NAMES: In French-Canada it's *Chouette-cendrée*—"Ashen Owl"—but in France and most of Europe it is Lapland Owl. To Germans it is *Bartkauz*, "Bearded Owl," in token of the black chin patch outlined in white. One of its many Amerindian names is *nuhl-tuhl*, "one who moves heavily"—probably referring to its slowness in taking flight rather than weight since this species is the lightest of the three Supers.

● ID CLUES: Size—length 24-33 inches; wingspan 50-60 inches. Head—round, large. Eyes—yellow, smaller than for other Supers; surrounding discs wider and more marked. Coloring—smoky gray streaked in darker gray with some white streaks on chest.

● HABITAT: Dense forests, coniferous or hardwood, especially pine, spruce, paper birch, poplar. Often near water or marsh. Uses nests of hawks, ravens or made-to-order imitations.

Snowy Owl, Sir William Jardine.

SNOWY OWL, *Nyctea scandiaca*

The label of Scandinavian Nightbird seemed right to Swedish classifier Carl Linnaeus in 1758. But owlers now know Snowy is at home in all northern lands the world around. Also it is far more active in daytime than owls farther south unaccustomed to the 24-hour days of Arctic summers. When food is scarce in Arctic winters Snowies wander south and have even strayed as far as Texas and other Gulf Coast states on a few occasions. One such wanderer was treated by a veterinarian for a wounded wing and is now on record as the only owl patient to eat a mouse right out of the freezer. All other owls treated there have waited for frozen food to thaw, but Snowies have evidently dined on ice-hard flesh before.

● FOLK NAMES: Arctic Owl, Ermine or Ghost Owl, Great White Owl, Terror of the North.

● OTHER NAMES: Most European names mean Snow Owl. Norwegians call it Lemming Owl and Swedes Highland Tundra Owl.

- **ID CLUES:** Size—length 20-30 inches; wingspan 51-70 inches. Head—round, large. Eyes—yellow. Coloring—speckled white, female more speckled than male for camouflage on nest.
- **HABITAT:** Tundra, especially where earth mounds and rocks provide some shelter. On winter wandering—meadows, marshes, sandy beaches. Nests on ground in a hollow or a-top a mound.

Two Are Large

Barred Owl, John James Audubon.

BARRED OWL, *Strix varia*

A "varied" or mottled plumage is typical of this species as it is of most owls. It also has the big head and distinct facial discs that place it in genus *Strix* where it has been since American naturalist Benjamin Barton classified it in 1799. However, it is no longer strictly an eastern species as it used to be and is now seen in much of the west. Southern plantation folk used to interpret its call as asking "Who cooks for you? Who cooks for you all?"—as if trying to decide which household might serve the best scraps for owl picnics. Others hear it as "More rain for you, more rain for you all!" It also seems to be challenging any owl intruder with "Who's hooting round here? Who's hooting right now?" Or how does it sound to you?

In the west it is now the rival of the Spotted Owl.

● FOLK NAMES: Hooting Owl, Swamp Owl. Woods Owl, Rain Owl, Round-headed Owl. Europeans mistake it for the Tawny Owl.

● OTHER NAMES: In French Canada it is *Chouette Rayée,* "Striped Owl," or *Chat-huant,* "Hooting Cat."

● ID CLUES: Size—length 16-24 inches; wingspan 38-45 inches. Head—round. Eyes—dark. Coloring—mottled brown on wings and back, barred (horizontal) lines under chin but striped (vertical) lines from chest to crotch in contrast to the Spotted which is barred all the way down.

● HABITAT: Dense woodlands, coniferous or hardwood, and in the south live oak or cabbage palm, usually near water or marsh. Nests in tree and rock cavity or old crow or hawk nest or in nest box 13x15x16 inches with entry hole 8 inches in diameter.

Spotted Owl, *Encyclopedia Britannica,* 1910.

SPOTTED OWL, *Strix occidentalis*

"Westerner" is still the word for the Spotted Owl as it

was in 1869 when Hungarian refugee Janos Xántus (who also used the surname de Vesey) found this owl in Fort Tejon, California, while serving there with the U.S. Army. Xántus sent many bird specimens to the Smithsonian including five species not then classified. For this new owl he chose genus *Syrnium*—Latinized version of an old Greek word for owls meaning "bird of ill omen." Later classifiers put it in genus *Strix* where it still stands.

● FOLK NAMES: Hooting Owl, Woods Owl, Western Barred Owl, Xántus' Owl, Canyon Owl, Arizona Spotted Owl.

● OTHER NAMES: In addition to its many Indian names it is known in Mexico as *tecolote manchado*—which adds the Spanish for "spotted" to Aztec term for all large owls.

● ID CLUES: Size—length 15-24 inches; wingspan 37-44 inches. Head—rounded. Eyes—dark. Coloring—mottled brown on wings and back with barred (horizontal) lines from chin to crotch.

● HABITAT: Dense forest, especially old-growth fir, and wooded, steep-walled canyons. Nests in tree cavity, prefers old-growth Douglas; will occasionally use rock cavity.

Four of Medium Size

COMMON BARN-OWL, *Tyto alba*

This far-ranging owl had collected hundreds of names in hundreds of languages before the Italian naturalist Giovanni Scopoli provided its first official listing as *Strix alba* in 1769. As more and more scientists realized one genus was not enough for owls, re-classification was sure to follow for this species with the pointed chin, and eventually the old nickname *Tyto* was chosen.

Its pale feathering and eerie voice are responsible for its widespread reputation as phantom, evil spirit, bringer of death warnings. And the eerie aura is augmented when an owl has been roosting among rotting wood coated with a phosphorescent glow which is absorbed by its feathers, adding mystery beyond mystery for watchers who see the

Common Barn-Owl, Alexander Wilson.

pale glow wavering through the air on ghostly wings. Almost as persistent is its fame as a destroyer of rats and mice. Over and over in the old books—and in many new ones—it is pictured with rat in claws or mouse in beak. Other owls catch rats, too, but the Common Barn-Owl has the big reputation for super-service.

It also has the name of one who defends its home with unequaled ferocity. Even the 16th century Franciscan naturalist, Bernardino de Sahagún, felt he must add warning: "It will claw you!"

● FOLK NAMES: Golden Owl, Silver Owl, White Owl, Ghost Owl, Demon Owl, Hissing Owl.

● OTHER NAMES: German *Schleiereule*, "Mystery or Phantom Owl," French *Chouette Effraie*, "Ill-omen Owl," Swedish *Tornuggla*, "Belfry Owl," Dutch *Kerkuil*, "Church Owl," Spanish *Lechuza* (echoic) or *Autillo*, "Knows-all," English "Screech-Owl," "Hobby Owl" (i.e. hobgoblin), "Monkey-faced Owl."

● ID CLUES: Size—length 14-21 inches; wingspan 40-45 inches. Head—round, but pointed chin, heart-shaped face. Eyes—dark. Coloring—comes in two phases. More common phase has white or very pale front, light buffy-yellow wings and back. Darker phase has buffy-yellow front and back, or even an almost orange-buffy shade.

● HABITAT: Open country, farms, villages, often nests in steeples, buildings of all kinds as well as barns and in rock crevices and tree cavities. Evidently the abundance of rodent food around farms leads it to nest there so often. Has nested in Wood-Duck boxes, also in niches intended for tame pigeons. Does not harm other pigeons if nesting in same loft, evidently preferring to keep its home area free from reprisal. Wood-Duck box is 18x18x24 with 4-inch hole 3 or 4 inches from top.

Northern Hawk-Owl, John James Audubon.

NORTHERN HAWK-OWL, *Surnia ulula*

In 1758 Linnaeus classified this slender, long-tailed owl in genus *Strix* with more typical owls and borrowed echoic Latin more often applied to the Barn-Owl as species label. As classifying became more detailed, a new genus was needed and in 1806 French naturalist Dumeril chose *surnia*, Latinized from Greek *syrnion*, "bird of ill omen," another borrowing from the Barn-Owl.

Hawk-Owls do have a harsh scream and quavery cry to warrant *ulula* naming, though their voices—like shape and flight pattern—are more hawklike than owlish. They are well known as day-fliers in lands all around the North

Pole, but seldom go far south even in harsh winters and so were not the villains of as many tales of "ill omen" as other owls. Watch any Accipter hawk scouting for prey and you'll know how the Hawk-Owl looks in pursuit of a meal. If you also see the eyes-front owl face, you'll know you've found *Surnia ulula,* the owl that isn't completely an owl. It's seldom on Christmas Bird Counts south of the Canadian border but has been recorded once or twice in Washington, North Dakota, Minnesota, Wisconsin, Michigan and New York.

● FOLK NAMES: Canadian Owl, Day Owl, Sparrowhawk Owl, Falcon Owl, Hudsonian Owl, Stub Owl (because it nests in broken-top tree stubs).

● OTHER NAMES: In Dutch, French and German it is Sparrow Owl but to Italians it is *Ulula.*

● ID CLUES: Size—length 14-17½ inches; wingspan 30-35 inches. Head—round, cheeks heavily outlined in black. Eyes—yellow. Coloring—horizontal barring on breast and belly distinguish it from smaller Boreal Owl and long tail sets it apart from equally barred Spotted Owl; also has more white on back and wings than Spotted, especially farther north where snow lingers.

● HABITAT: Open forests or forest edges, tamarack and muskeg swamps, areas with thick underbrush. Nests in tree cavities, old crow nests, sometimes in rock cavities.

SHORT-EARED OWL, *Asio flammeus*

"Flame-colored" is a bit of hyperbole Danish naturalist Erik Pontoppidan chose to apply with his *Strix flammeus* label in 1763. "Buff-colored" would have been a more helpful clue, for this species does have buff patches other brown owls lack. However, "short-eared" is right to the point, for the tufts are definitely short, at times even difficult to see. It is in genus *Asio* because it is so much like a Long-eared Owl that the two have to be in the same genus. (See next entry for Long-eared Owl.)

Short-eared Owls choose to nest on the ground in

Short-eared Owl, Sir William Jardine.

meadows and marshes rather than in tree and rock cavities, an important clue to their identification. Like other ground-nesters they can put on quite a lame-wing, oh-so-helpless act to lure you away from eggs or owlets, but then take off hissing and snapping and hovering well out of reach—from your hands or mammal's leap but not from guns—when you come too close.

To warn rival owls too near boundary lines, they give alarm by clapping their wings together—sharply, below the belly—with a sound that can be heard from a remarkable distance. A potential mate understands its message, too, and may therefore clearly see the area a suitor offers. In these overcrowded times, ground nesters are more vulnerable to attack from hungry predators and to disruption by humans needing more ground themselves for homes and highways and other structures, and so Short-eared Owls have vanished from some areas, become scarce in others. Lately they have been seen roosting in tree-tops—often moving to trees already occupied by a Long-earned Owl or two for winter roost. So far, they have not begun nesting in trees. Could that be the next step for preservation of the species? Only careful check by owlers will give the answer.

In the Hawaiian Islands, the native Short-eared Owl subspecies *Asio flammeus sandwichensis* has no Long-eared kin to copy and is declining alarmingly. Introduced predators, including feral cats and Barn-Owls, may be partly responsible. Formerly common on all Main Islands and on Kaui and Maui, especially in Haleakala Crater and in grassy areas near towns. Only occasionally on islands of Northwest Chain. In 1987 nests reported only from Oahu. (Subspecies name is from Sandwich Islands, first English name for Hawaii)

● FOLK NAMES: Grass Owl, Marsh Owl, Meadow Owl, Bog Owl, Swamp Owl (in Florida, Palmetto Owl) Flat-faced Owl, Woodcock Owl (because they return from migration at same date).

● OTHER NAMES: In most European languages it is the equivalent of Marsh Owl, as in French it is *Hibou des Marais*. In Hawaii it is *Pueo*.

● ID CLUES: Size—length 13-17 inches; wingspan 38-44 inches. Head—short erectile tufts. Eyes—yellow, encircled by black splotches. Coloring—in flight, large buffy patches show on upperside of wings, on underside dark patch near wrist joint (bend of wing) basic color under streaking much buffier than for other owls.

● HABITAT: Open country, especially near marshes, often near airports where land is kept free of buildings. Nests on ground in shelter of mound or grass clump.

LONG-EARED OWL, *Asio otus*

The genus label *asio*—"asslike"—was first given to this species by the Roman naturalist Pliny to compare its long tufts—longest of all owl species—to floppy donkey ears. Eventually it also burdened the owl with a reputation for asslike stupidity. Several centuries earlier Aristotle had simply used Greek for "eared"—*otis*. In 1758 Linnaeus

Long-eared Owl, Alexander Wilson.

published it as *Strix otus,* Latinizing Aristotle's term and using the same genus he gave all owls. French classifier Mathurin Brisson added Latin to Greek to coin the present label *Asio otus* in 1760—which presented no problem until English naturalist Thomas Pennant re-named our Eastern Screech-Owl with the reverse combination, *Otus asio.*

If you care enough about scientific labels to want help in remembering which bird gets which tag, try this: when *asio* comes before *otus,* the ears are longer. And if you think it stupid to call an owl an ass, remember the mule deer of western North America was named for the same long-eared reason.

Almost every description of the Long-eared Owl—all the way back to Belon and Gesner in 1555—comments on these longest owl tufts. Even though they are erectile, they're usually up full length for the one clue you can't miss. You may also note Long-eareds do not use wing-clap signal like the Short-eared and are tree nesters and tree perchers more often than ground birds.

● FOLK NAMES: Brush Owl, Lesser Horned Owl, Cat Owl.

- OTHER NAMES: French *Moyen Duc,* German *Waldoh-reule* "Woods Owl," Swedish *Hornuggla,* "Horned Owl."
- ID CLUES: Size—length 13-16 inches; wingspan 36-43 inches. Head—tufts erect, long, more to center of head than tufts of Great Horned or Screech-Owls. Eyes—yellow-orange, feathers around eyes are buffy-orange rather than the black of Short-eared, although there is black between eyes and beak. Coloring—streaked brown, more gray in streaking than buff of Short-eared.
- HABITAT: Woods near water, likes thick undergrowth, sometimes roosts or nests in caves and rock crevices. In nesting season each pair keeps to itself, but often migrate in groups and gather at winter roost with as many as 15 or 20 birds together, sometimes including Short-eared Owls.

Four Small Owls

BOREAL OWL, *Aegolius funereus*

The "funereal owl" label given by Linnaeus in 1758 is still part of the scientific label although this is no more a "death owl" than any other Strigiformes and certainly has much less claim to such crepe-hanging than the Barn-Owl in world lore and legend. Johann Gmelin tried to amend the misnomer by labeling it Tengmalm's Owl and it is still so called in Europe. British-Americans named it for one of their own explorers, Richardson's Owl, and both names are still in older books. Meanwhile the German naturalist Johann Kaup applied the generic label *Aegolius,* "goatlike," harking back to all the old tales of nightbirds chasing goats to steal a sip of milk and to the goatlike whiskery feathers on many an owl face. The bristly white of the feathers around the chin of this species may look more like goat whiskers than similar touches on other owl faces or they may not. The term "Boreal" marks this owl's northern range in Europe and Asia as well as Canada and Alaska and a few mountainous areas farther south along the Rockies.

This northerner has an unusual tinkling call that sounds like drops of water splashing into a pool from some trickling streamlet and then swishing away as the pool overflows into a larger stream. At least that's how it sounded to Montagnais Indians long ago, and to the French trappers who wrote it down with "pee-leep-pee-lay-tsschish" echo. And they also re-told the old Quebec Indian legend explaining that this ten-inch owl was once the largest of all owls, with a booming voice to match its bulk. It was so proud of its loud cries that it even challenged the largest waterfall in the land to a contest as to which of them could drown out the other. As it happened, the waterfall was sacred to the Great Spirit who promptly punished the owl for its temerity by shrinking it in size and turning its voice into mere ting-a-ling chime.

Actually, the Boreal's small size is an advantage, for it needs less food than larger northerners such as the Snowy and Great Gray and so can stay north most winters instead of having to migrate in search of prey. However, Boreals do occasionally turn up in Maine and Massachusetts, Colorado and all states close to the Canadian border. Less often they go farther south and at least one reached New Mexico in 1987. They now nest occasionally in Washington, Oregon, New York and probably other places yet to be verified. It's definitely a species to look for an owl safari.

- FOLK NAMES: Sparrow Owl.
- OTHER NAMES: Some Eskimos call it *Tuckwellinguk,* the blind one," thinking poor eyesight must be the reason it is so easily approached to arm's length.
- ID CLUES: Size—8-12 inches; wingspan 19½-26 inches— noticeably smaller than the Hawk Owl with somewhat similar range and markings. Head—round. Eyes—yellow. Coloring—beneath the white speckling the Boreal has a reddish-brown cast that might be confused with the Saw-whet, but the Boreal has a blacker, wider facial outline, and no reddish facial tint.
- HABITAT: Dense forests, alder thickets, spruce clumps

near meadows. Nests in old woodpecker holes, especially in conifers.

Burrowing Owl, Titian Peale.

BURROWING OWL, *Athene cunicularia*

Burrowing Owls were once thought to be exclusively American with no close Old World relatives. An Italian Jesuit in Chile—J. Ignacio Molina—was first to classify them in 1782, choosing the specific name *cunicularia*— "rabbit-like"—because both birds and bunnies live in underground burrows. Later classifiers took it out of the catch-all genus *Strix* Molina had chosen and coined a new term, *Speyotyto*, combining an old word for "cave" with an old name for Barn-Owls. The Burrowers do resemble the name-source species in having long rather awkward-looking legs and a round head, but in little else. More recent classifiers have seen closer anatomical likeness to *Athene noctua*, the famous Little Owl of old Athens, and so since 1983 it has been in genus *Athene* with *noctua* and only two other Old World species.

This is one species you can identify by its choice of homesite without much question. They can dig their burrow themselves, but usually prefer to take over a suitable tunnel abandoned by prairie dogs, rabbits, armadillos, gophers, badgers. Since these tunnels also suit rattlesnakes, the two have similar quarters but do not share the same diggings as has often been claimed. That rumor probably got its start because the warning signal given by Burrower nestlings is almost identical with a snake's rattle. The parent on watch topside at the tunnel door scoots down instantly to remedy whatever is amiss and if there are humans to see and hear, the rumor is fortified once again.

Over-curious humans who have tried to dig into a tunnel to see what goes on have reported attacks by Papa Burrower with batting wings and slashing claws and beak. If retreat isn't prompt, every other male in the colony may join the attack, while females tend to gather in a group and do the owl equivalent of wringing their hands. Or so the claim goes.

Much more reliable is the story that these owls hunt through the winter while the weather is good, storing surplus rodents and other edibles in an underground chamber to eat when ice or snow prevents hunting. On sunny days year round they may be sitting by the door-way—or standing on one leg, resting the other under warm feathers—bobbing their heads from side to side and back and forth in order to judge the distance kept by any approaching stranger and meanwhile looking as solemn as the proverbial judge.

• FOLK NAMES: Billy Owl, Howdy Owl (because the head bobing looks like friendly greeting), Cuckoo Owl (it has a cuckoo-like call, also called dovelike), plus the names of all the animals whose homes they borrow—(gopher owl, etc.).

• OTHER NAMES: Spanish-speaking Americans from Mexico to Chile often call it *Lechucillo*, diminutive of their name for the Barn-Owl. It also has numerous names in Indian languages.

● ID CLUES: Size—8-11 inches; wingspan 22-24 inches. Head—round. Eyes—yellow. Coloring—basic brown well sprinkled with white, broad white bib under chin.

● HABITAT: Prairies, grasslands with dry sandy soil easily excavated, airports, farm lands not in cultivation. Although always more common in the west and south-west, individuals have been seen in northern and eastern areas recently from Virginia to Massachusetts and one adventurer was seen on Martha's Vineyard. It also nests in the Midwest more often than before, expansion probably due to overcrowding humans in former territory. Also many thriving colonies in Florida since first seen near Sarasota in 1874. These colonies are moving out in all directions, even farther north and west.

Screech-Owl, Alexander Wilson.

EASTERN SCREECH-OWL, *Otus asio*
WESTERN SCREECH-OWL, *Otus kennicotti*

Western and Eastern Screech-owls have been considered separate species only since 1983 although the western species has been identified since 1867. For years various subspecies have been published, most of them west of the Mississippi River. These now come under the *kennicotti* label when only full species are considered.

The main difference between Eastern and Western species is that easterners customarily have reddish plumage as often as gray, even in the same family, while Western Screech-Owls are almost always gray. Also, most of the western owls are slightly larger. Both are smaller than other tufted North American owls except the Whiskered Screech-Owl and Flammulated Owls, which are both among the smallest owl group.

Western Screech-Owls have a different call, a bouncing "woo, wu-wu-wu, woo-oo!" while the Eastern usually gives a quavery tremulous wail. In border areas where both species may be seen you will want to listen for identification rather than merely look. Both species are often the Gray Owl or Little Horned Owl in Indian legends and superstition. Seminole Indians, for instance, still remember the old Screech-Owl Dance, with one dancer representing the owl with gourd in hand to give a touch of magic while other men and women hold hands for step and stomp in traditional circle chain. Among Louisiana Cajuns there are superstitions that involve Screech-Owls, too. If you hear the wailing call some dark night you can avert whatever evil or disaster is predicted by owl presence, old timers say, by getting up from bed and turning over your left shoe so it is upside-down.

● FOLK NAMES: Little Horned Owl, Dusk Owl, Ghost Owl, Shoe Owl, Little Cat Owl, Death Owl, Whining Owl, Wailing Owl, Mouse Owl and almost any other folk name for larger tufted owls.

● OTHER NAMES: In Spanish it is *Tecolotito,* the diminutive of the echoic name for the Great Horned Owl, or less often *Chillon Encinero*, "Ash-colored Screamer," a name for Barn-Owls as well as Screech-owls.

• ID CLUES: Size—length 7-12 inches (Western), 7-10 (Eastern) wingspan 19-23½ inches (Western) 18-23 inches (Eastern). Head—tufted (Western and Eastern). Eyes—yellow (Western and Eastern). Coloring—streaked, mottled gray or rufous.

• HABITAT: Woodlands, oak and other deciduous trees in wilds or parks or suburban backyards, often near water. Will use nest box 8x8x12 inches with 3-inch entry hole 2-3 inches from top of box. Nests in old woodpecker holes, often in orchards.

Six of the Very Smallest

WHISKERED SCREECH-OWL, *Otus trichopsis*

"One with ears and whiskers" is the meaning of this Latin label. When Johann Wagler of Munich chose *trichopsis* in 1832 he may or may not have known how many others through the years had thought of owls as hairy-faced, bearded, with mustache or whiskers rather than feathers. Few others in those days had seen this owl whose more usual haunts are in Mexico. The same shipment of specimens from Mexico had brought him the Northern Pygmy-Owl also and Wagler must have wondered if most of the owls from the Americas were so small. Even today it is not seen much farther north than the border areas of Arizona and New Mexico, so it is not on many owling lists.

If you see it without an Eastern or Western Screech-Owl handy for size comparison, the two inches or so difference may not be easily noticed. But it will be about in daytime more often than the others, for it has good day vision. Also you may hear a courting male and his mate give their question-and-answer duet—her two-note trill somewhat higher in pitch than his but both musical, both tremulous. At other times their calls tend to have six or eight hoots.

- FOLK NAMES: Spotted Screech-Owl.

- OTHER NAMES: In Mexico it is *Tecolotito,* like most small owls, but sometimes *Manchado,* "spotted" or *Llanero,* "of the plains," is added—the latter a misnomer since it prefers high country.

- ID CLUES: Size—6½—7½ inches; wingspan 15-21 inches. Head—tufted. Eyes—yellow. Coloring—may come in red phase like other Screech-Owls but gray more common and more heavily splotched in white; white bib under chin noticeable and may have been part of the reason for "whisker" label.

- HABITAT: Prefers oak-grove canyons and slopes, may avoid denser conifer stands to escape Great Horned Owls, seldom goes into lowlands. Nests in tree cavities, old woodpecker holes.

Saw-whet Owl, John James Audubon.

NORTHERN SAW-WHET OWL, *Aegolius acadicus*

Its common name is due to a raspy voice that sounded—at least to oldtime lumbermen—like someone sharpening a mill saw. English birder George Latham gave it specific label for "Acadian" since he first saw it in the Canadian border lands that once went by that name. Johann Gmelin crammed it into genus *Strix,* of course—the only category for owls in 1788—and it would be some years before it was placed in genus *Aegolius*. That's Latinized-Greek for "goatlike" and therefore is another notch on the long stick marking goat-and-owl mix-up.

Although Saw-whet Owls still roam Acadia they are also at home all across the continent. Although they nest all the way to southern Alaska along the west coast and to Hudson Bay on the east, many individuals go south for the winter. Like the Snowy, they delight owlers all across the land by turning up unexpectedly. Like the Snowy and most other owls that seldom see many people on their nesting grounds, they are usually easy to approach on winter wanderings and so often join the others in being labeled too trusting for their own good.

In October 1986 over 421 southbound Saw-whets were banded in one night at Prince Edward Point on Lake Ontario and another 126 were banded at Long Point on Lake Erie another night and still 181 more at Prince Edward Point on another night. Where they all went after that is not on record, but one Saw-whet did turn up in Alabama in January. Owlers believe many more of these little russet-feathered owls go far southward and escape unnoticed simply because they are so small and so quiet during winter months. Good advice to the rest of us—keep looking for the owl from Acadia that may be as much a wanderer as Longfellow's Evangeline, also from that storied land.

● FOLK NAMES: Acadian Owl, Sparrow Owl, Kirtland's Owl.

● OTHER NAMES: French Canada, *Petite Nyctale*, "Little Nightbird," or *Chouette des Granges*, "Farmland Owl."

● ID CLUES: Size—length 7-8 inches; wingspan 18-22 inches. Head—round, big. Eyes—yellow. Coloring—less splotched with white on wings and back than Boreal Owl (which is also larger) has much less white on face than Boreal and has russet face-markings which Boreal lacks and does not have Boreal's distinct black facial outline. Saw-whet is much more streaked with white on belly than

Boreal. Has short tail in comparison with long-tailed Pygmy-Owls of same russet hue.

● HABITAT: Dense forests, groves, thickets either coniferous or hardwood, tamarack bogs. In winter wanderings may often take shelter in buildings. Will use nest-box if provided with sawdust, shavings, straw—try 7x7x12 inch box with 2½ inch entry hole 2-3 inches from top. Also tree cavities.

FLAMMULATED OWL, *Otus flammeolus*

Touches of russet or cinnamon feathering—not flame— give this small western owl its misleading name. But that's no problem for owlers catching their first glimpse. Dark eyes—not the more usual yellow ones—distinguish the Flammulated Owl at a glance. As the only Small or Very Small Owl in North America with dark eyes, it's sure to be identified correctly. However, because it is seen only in the Far West, it was late in being classified. German naturalist Johann Kaup put it on record in 1853 but no nest was described till 1875.

Although it is now in genus *Otus* with the Screech-Owls, it does not have their easily-seen tufts. Instead, there is a little patch of longer dark feathers interrupting the facial outline above each eye. Call it a half-tuft, although there are plenty of times when it doesn't seem like a tuft at all. For another clue, look for a fair sprinkling of cinnamon on the facial discs which similar gray-feathered owls lack.

Finding this species in the first place may often take you considerably longer than identifying it once you see it. It ranges the Rockies from British Columbia to Guatemala and keeps fairly close to high-country woodlands. Both size and coloring enable it to blend in with the tree trunk where it sleeps by day and with the twilight mists. Consequently even oldtime owlers do not know much about its habits and even newcomers to owling art can be discoverers. However, the species does a lot of calling, especially in mating season. The usual call has two notes—as if the male is declaring *Two HOOTS! Two HOOTS!* and thereby proving to the listening female he cares for her the required amount.

Outside of mating season, their hooting is that of master ventriloquists and trying to locate the bird by its call can get you anywhere except the branch on which the hooter is sitting. If that makes you think "Flim-flam Owl" is an apt nickname, it's one of the few the official name engenders.

- FOLK NAMES: Dwarf Owl.
- OTHER NAMES: In French Canada *Petit Duc Nain*, "Little Dwarf Duke." In Mexico *Tecolotito,* "Little Owl."
- ID CLUES: Size—length 6-7 inches; wingspan 14½-19½ inches. Head—half tufts, not always visible. Eyes—dark (best clue). Coloring—has less-seen red phase as well as usual gray phase with cinnamon highlights on face and wings—a nice combination of salt-and-pepper-with-cinnamon.
- HABITAT: Keeps to high country, rare in lowlands. Prefers deep thickets near more open country for hunting, often in pine and oak, less often in madrona, pinon. May sometimes take over an abandoned shack or tool shed. Nests in crow nest, old woodpecker holes.

Pygmy-Owl, Harry Fosbury.

NORTHERN PYGMY-OWL, *Glaucidium gnoma*
FERRUGINOUS PYGMY-OWL, *Glaucidium brasilianum*

These two small ones with russet coats are so much alike that the best way to know them is to consider them together. The Ferruginous is slightly smaller and was discovered first—in Brazil—and so bears species name *brasilianum* bestowed by Johann Gmelin in 1788. Its more northern congener was not recorded until 1832 and is indebted to Johann Wagler for first listing and "gnome" label. The genus name was applied first to European species and marks the typical bright yellow eyes with a form of *glaux*, the same Greek word that once named Athena's nightbird with the shining eyes.

Seven species from the Old World and five from the New share *Glaucidium* genus. Besides these two there is one each from Cuba, Equador and Mexico and all are in Very Small category by owl standards. However, when a Northern Pygmy came flitting into an Oregon patio one winter day, it suddenly loomed large beside the patio's tiny defender. Challenging its right to shelter was one super-belligerent Anna's Hummingbird with a temper to match its fire-red helmet as it swooped and swirled in dive-bomb attack. The Pygmy countered with feathers fluffed out twice its size, but the long hummer beak slashed through, and the owl—eyes wide in what must have been amazed wonder—departed never to return. Like most small owls, it may have killed its share of warblers, chickadees and such, but this could have been its first encounter with a hummingbird beak. And maybe its last. Birds do learn—and revise life styles accordingly.

Both Northern and Ferruginous share the same basic coloring that gave the latter its name. Both share the same body shape, same yellow eyes, same long tail. To tell them apart, look first at the back between nape and rump—for the Ferruginous it's plain reddish all the way. For the Northern the same area is heavily speckled in white, and its dark tail is barred in white also. The Ferruginous tail is its name color barred in smoky black.

Both also share a camouflage marking that has no doubt helped many an individual stay alive. You'll see it at a glance—two black ovals bordered in white like two big eyes in the back of the head! So these two seem to have their eyes on you no matter where you are and many a hopeful predator must have turned away thinking it had already been noticed, no use to linger. As it happens, both Pygmies also see well in both daylight and dark so they have added advantage other owls lack.

The Northerner ranges through the west from British Columbia to Guatemala, while the Ferruginous rarely comes up over the Mexican border. However, extending former boundaries seems to be standard procedure lately for both species—the Northern has reached Alaska and the Ferruginous may be getting ready to add California's southern edges to those of Texas, New Mexico and Arizona.

● FOLK NAMES, OTHER NAMES: In all languages, "pygmy" seems to be name and nickname enough. In areas where both appear, the Ferruginous is the Desert Pygmy and the Northern the Mountain Pygmy. Any other tags haven't had much use.

● ID CLUES: Northern Size—length 6-7½ inches; wingspan 14-15½ inches. Head—rounded. Eyes—yellow. Coloring— back between nape and rump and tail coloring are clues, see above for both species. Ferruginous Size—length 5½-7 inches; wingspan 14-16 inches. Head, Eyes, Coloring—as above.

• HABITAT: For Northern mostly mountain forests near water, though at sea level along the Pacific Coast in thickets and brush, trees as available. For Ferruginous saguaro and cholla cactus, mesquite stands, likes dense foliage for roosts, often along creeks. Both use old woodpecker holes.

ELF OWL, *Micrathene whitneyi*

The genus choice—Tiny Athene—marks the small size of this smallest owl north of Mexico. The species name honors Josiah Dwight Whitney, mining geologist, graduate of Yale and a professor at Harvard, who helped his friend Dr. James Gordon Cooper with birding while both were stationed in California in the 1860s. This particular namesake specimen came from Fort Mohave, Arizona, and it is still more likely to be found in Arizona than anywhere else north of the border, although it is also seen in the states on either side and in Texas as well.

In contrast to the rusty-hued, long-tailed Pygmy-Owls, the Elf is sandy colored and bob-tailed. You may not believe any owl could be so small until you actually see it, but once you have it in sight you know it has to be the Elf. Most writers mark its small build by measuring it sparrow-size, but one author—Allan Eckert in his *The Owls of North America*—takes the unbelievable step further and declares it could perch comfortably on your soda-straw. And it does weigh barely an ounce, so a straw may serve.

It feeds on insects and other invertebrates for the most part but will now and then be able to snag a small mouse or shrew, perhaps even a bird smaller than itself. Somehow it has learned the trick of going limp whenever a human clutches one in hand, feigning death as expertly as any opossum and springing back to action with incredible agility the moment the hand relaxes its grip, disappearing with quick wing flip. "Playing Elf" you might say the next time you have an occasion to comment on death-sham defense. It has also learned that humans and other enemies often do not see whatever does not move and so it "freezes" with instant immovability until danger passes by.

- FOLK NAMES, OTHER NAMES: Like the Pygmy-Owls, the Elf seems to have the only name it needs. In Mexico it is *Enano*, "Dwarf," accenting small size, rather than *Duende* which would mark it a mischief-making hobgoblin.
- ID CLUES: Size—length 5-6½ inches; wingspan 13½-15 inches. Head—round. Eyes—yellow. Coloring—color shades may run from buff to sandy to almost gray depending on area, whitish "whiskers" of eyebrows meet at the center to run down along each side of the beak to the chin. Basic color and tail length distinguish it from Pygmy-Owls, roundness of head—no hint of even half tufts—separates even the gray color phase from the Flammulated Owl and from the well-tufted Whiskered Screech-Owl.
- HABITAT: Desert with giant cacti or woodlands near water. Nests in old woodpecker holes in saguaro cactus, mesquite, pine, oak, sycamore or in natural cavities.

So runs the tally from largest to smallest, from over two feet in length to under a half-foot, but all with eyes front above rounded cheeks in a visage that marks the owls and no others among all those in feathers.

Bibliography

Allen, Robert. *Birds of the Caribbean.* New York: Viking, 1961

American Birds. National Audubon Society, New York. Articles on distribution in all issues. Christmas Bird Count results, July-August issues.

American Ornithologists' Union. *Check-list of North American Birds.* Washington, D.C. Sixth Edition 1983.

Armstrong, Edward. *Life and Lore of the Bird.* New York: Crown, 1975.

___*Folklore of Birds.* Boston: Houghton Mifflin, 1958.

Arno Hermanos. *Catalog de las Vocas Usuales de Aimara, Castellano y Quechua.* La Paz, Bolivia: Arno Hermanos, 1944.

Audubon, John James. Birds of America, volume 1. New York: Audubon & Chevalier, 1840-44; Dover Publications, Inc. 1966.

Belon, Pierre. *L'Histoire de la Nature des Oyseaux.* Paris: Chez Guillaume Cavellat, 1555.

Benson, S. Vere. *The Observer's Book of British Birds.* London: Frederick Warne & Co. Ltd. 1952.

Bent, Arthur Cleveland. *Life Histories of North American Birds of Prey, Part Two.* Washington, D.C.: U.S. National Museum Bulletin 170, 1938. Reprint, Dover, 1961.

Berger, Andrew J. *Bird Life in Hawaii.* Honolulu: Island Heritage Press, 1983.

Bond, James. *Birds of the West Indies.* Boston: Houghton Mifflin, 1980.

Bowes, Anne L. *Birds of the Mayas.* Big Moose, N.Y.: West-of-the-Wind Publications, 1964.

Bull, Evelyn and Mark Henjum. "The Neighborly Great Gray Owl," *Natural History,* September 1987. New York: American Museum of Natural History.

Catesby, Mark. *Natural History of Carolina, Florida and the Bahama Islands.* London: 1731-43. Self published.

Colton, Harold S. *Hopi Kachina Dolls.* Albuquerque, N.M.: University of New Mexico Press, 1959.

Cordam, Marty and Annette. "Spotted Owl." *Animals,* August 1983. Boston: Massachusetts S.P.C.A.

Curtis, Natalie, *The Indians' Book.* New York: Dover Publications, 1968.

De Armas, Juan Ignacio. La Zoologia de Colon y de los Primeros Exploradores de America. Havana, Cuba: Tipografico O'Reilly 1888.

Eckert, Allan W. *Owls of North America.* New York: Weathervane Books, 1987.

Elbert, Samuel and Mary Kawena Pukui. *Hawaiian Enlgish Dictionary.* Honolulu: University of Hawaii Press, 1965.

Gesner, Konrad. *Historiae animalium, lib III . . . de avium.* Zurich: 1555.

Grimm, Jacob and Wilhelm. *Fairy Tales.* New York: Pantheon Books, 1944.

Grossman, Mary Louise and John Hamlet. *Birds of Prey of the World.* New York: Clarkson Potter, Inc. 1964.

Hannon, Buck L. "A Hoot for the Home," *Northwest Magazine,* August 8, 1976. Portland, Oregon: The Oregonian Publishing Co.

Harris, Clement, "Musical Animals in Ornament." *Musical Quarterly,* vol VI, pages 417-25. 1920.

Harris. J. and Howard Galbraith. "The Sauke Collection." *Screenings,* 9-9-1958. Portland, OR. The Oregon Archaeological Society.

Henninger, Jean, "Great Arctic Snowy Owl." *The Oregonian,* 11-30-77; "Wing Healed." *The Oregonian,* 1-7-78. Portland, OR.

Hernández, Francisco. *Cuatro libros de la naturaleza y virtudes medicinales de las plantas y animales y minerales de Neuvo Espana.* Mexico: 1615.

Holmgren, Virginia C. *Bird Walk Through the Bible.* New York: Seabury Press, 1972; Dover reprint, 1988.

——*Scans Key to Birdwatching.* Portland, OR.: Timber Press, 1983.

Hudson, W.H. *The Bird Biographies of W.H. Hudson.* Santa Barbara, CA. Capra Press 1988.

Jardine, Sir William. *The Naturalists' Library.* vol. 1 London/Edinburgh, 1830 (no date).

Konishi, Masakazu. "Night Owls Are Good Listerners." *Natural History,* September 1983. New York: American Museum of Natural History.

Laycock, George. *The Birdwatcher's Bible.* New York: Doubleday, 1976.

Lawson, John. *A New Voyage to Carolina.* London: 1709; edited with notes, Chapel Hill, N.C. University of North Carolina Press, 1967.

Linnaeus, Carl. *Systema Naturae.* Tenth Edition, Sweden, 1758.

Loring, J. Malcolm and Louise. *Pictographs and Petroglyphs of the Oregon Country.* Los Angeles: UCLA, 1982-83.

Lysaght, A.M. *The Book of Birds.* London: Phaidon Press, 1975.

MacRae, Diann. "Ten Raptor Books You Shouldn't Be Without". *Bird Watcher's Digest,* Sept/Oct 1987. Marietta, Ohio.

Maslow, Jonathan. *The Owl Papers.* New York: Dutton, 1983.

Medlin, Faith. *Centuries of Owls.* Norwalk, CN.: Silvermine Publishers, 1967.

Miller, Layne. "Rochester Creek, Utah." American Rock Art Research Association, American Indian Rock. vols 7/8, 1981.

Milne, Lorus J. and Margery. *The Senses of Animals and Men.* New York: Atheneum, 1964.

Monadori, Arnoldo, editor. *Uccelli d'Europa* (translated from Brunn, Bertel. *Hamlyn Guide to Birds of Britain and Europe)* Milano, 1975, 1980.

O'Neill, John P. and Gary R. Graves. "A New Genus and Species of Owl from Peru". *The Auk,* July 1977. Washington, D.C. The American Ornithologists' Union. 1977.

Palmer, Janet. "A Whoo's Whoo Birder Tells All". *Bird Watcher's Digest,* Sept/Oct 1987. Marietta, Ohio.

Pearse, Theed. *Birds of the Early Explorers in the Northern Pacific,* Comox, B.C.: Theed Pearse, 1968.

Peterson, Roger Tory et al. *A Field Guide to the Birds of Britain and Europe.* Boston: Houghton Mifflin. 1967.

Prescott, William. *A History of the Conquest of Mexico.* New York: Maynard, Merrell & Co. 1895; Modern Library reprint undated.

Rohweder, Ron. "Rare Owl." *Oregon Wildlife,* Feb. 1977. Portland, OR.: Oregon Dept. Fish & Wildlife.

Rowe, Matthew P. and Ted Wesemann, Anne Sisson. "Burrowing Owls in Florida's Urban Underground." *Bird Watcher's Digest,* Sept/Oct 1987. Marietta, Ohio.

Sahágun, Bernardino de. *Historia General de Cosas de Nuevo Espana.* Translated by C.E. Dibble and J.O. Anderson. Salt Lake City, UT. and Albuquerque, N.M. Presses of the Universities of Utah and New Mexico, 1963. (written ca. 1560).

Scott, Virgil E. et al. *Cavity-Nesting Birds of North American Forests.* Washington, D.C.: Agriculture Handbook 511, U.S. Forest Service. November 1977.

Shallenberger, R.J. et al. *Hawaii's Birds.* Honolulu: Hawaii Audubon Society, 1981.

Strong, Emory. *Stone Age on the Columbia.* Portland, OR.: Binford and Mort, 1959.

___"The John Krussow Collection," *Screenings,* 1-11-1960. Portland, OR.: The Oregon Archaeological Society.

Slatick, Eugene R. "Sharp Eyes: Bird Vision". *Oregon Wildlife,* Sept 1976. Portland, OR.: Oregon Dept. Fish & Wildlife.

Sparks, John and Tony Soper. *Owls.* New York: Taplinger, 1970.

Terres, John K. *The Audubon Encyclopedia of North American Birds.* New York: Knopf, 1980.

Thoreau, Henry David. *Walden.* Boston: Ticknow & Fields. 1854.

Townsend, John Kirk. *Narrative of a Journey Across the Rocky Mountains to the Columbia River.* Fairfield, WA.: Ye Galleon Press, 1976. Original Philadelphia 1839.

United States Bureau of Ethnology. *Annual Reports* 1879-1916. Washington, D.C.: Government Printing Office, 1879-1916.

Walls, G.L. "The vertebrate eye and its adaptive radiation." *Cranbrook Institute of Science Bulletin* #19. Bloomfield, Michigan: Cranbrook Inst. Sci. 1942.

Westervelt, W.D. *Hawaiian Legends of Old Honolulu.* Rutland, VT. and Tokyo, Japan: Charles E. Tuttle Company. no date.

Wetmore, Alexander. *Water, Prey and Game Birds.* Washington, D.C.: National Geographic Society, 1965.

Wilson, Alexander. *American Ornithology.* Philadelphia: Bradford & Inskeep, 1808-1813. Revision: Thomas Brewer, editor Boston: Otis, Broaders & Co. 1840; facsimile: New York: Arno Press, 1970.

Wolfe, Art. "Long-eared Owls, Masters of the Night." *National Georgraphic,* January, 1980. Washington, D.C.: National Geographic Society.

Wright, Barton. *Kachinas: A Hopi Artist's Documentary.* Flagstaff and Phoenix, AZ.: Northland Press and Heard Museum, 1973.

Long-eared Owl, Susemihl, Darmstadt, 1821.

Index

175